The Prince
Interpreted for Entrepreneurs

The Hard Truths About Power, Leadership, and Business Stability

ANCIENT WISDOM HACKS

Publisher: NX Inc

Third Edition

Table of Contents

Conclusion

Introduction

Purpose and Relevance

In a world where startups rise and fall with dizzying speed, the need for clear-eyed strategy has never been greater. Niccolò Machiavelli wrote *The Prince* over five centuries ago, yet his insights into power dynamics, human nature, and the art of adaptation remain uncannily relevant. As entrepreneurs navigate funding rounds, competitive threats, and shifting markets, they face challenges akin to those of Renaissance rulers defending their realms. Machiavelli's counsel—to "adapt yourself according to the times" and to recognize that "fortune is the ruler of one-half of our actions" —speaks directly to the modern founder's dilemma: how to seize opportunity, mitigate risk, and shape one's own destiny in an unpredictable landscape.

Why Machiavelli Still Matters to Modern Entrepreneurs

Machiavelli understood that authority is neither granted nor permanent—it must be earned and constantly renewed. He warned that "a prince who relies entirely on fortune goes down with it," emphasizing the importance of proactive leadership. For entrepreneurs, this translates into the imperative to build durable competitive advantages rather than rely solely on market hype or external funding. Machiavelli's pragmatic realism—his willingness to confront uncomfortable truths about loyalty, fear, and ambition—serves as both a guide and a cautionary tale. It reminds founders that charisma and vision must be backed by shrewd tactics and an unflinching assessment of the forces at play.

Translating Political Strategy into Business Strategy

At first glance, the court intrigues of Renaissance Italy may seem distant from lean startups and tech unicorns. Yet the core challenge remains: how to acquire, consolidate, and wield influence in a domain marked by rivals, shifting alliances, and the ever-present threat of disruption. Where Machiavelli advises a ruler to fortify cities and cultivate loyalty among the people, an entrepreneur must build resilient organizations and foster a culture that can withstand market turbulence. When *The Prince* counsels that "it is better to be feared than loved, if you cannot be both," it grapples with the tension between hard-nosed discipline and inspirational leadership—an equilibrium every founder must strike.

Understanding *The Prince*

Historical Context of Machiavelli's Work
Written in 1513 amid the fractious politics of Florence, *The Prince* was Machiavelli's response to exile and turmoil. Italy was a patchwork of city-states, each vying for advantage through shifting alliances, mercenary armies, and the machinations of powerful families. Machiavelli observed firsthand the fragility of power: one day a lord could command respect, the next be deposed or assassinated. This volatile environment birthed lessons in vigilance, adaptability, and the ruthless calculus of realpolitik—lessons that underpin every chapter of *The Prince*.

Core Themes: Power, Adaptation, Perception

1. **Power:** For Machiavelli, authority is not an abstract virtue but a tangible resource to be acquired, maintained, and, when necessary, wielded without scruple. He cautions against the naïve belief that moral goodness alone secures stability: "A prince must learn how not to be good, and to

use this knowledge or not according to necessity."

2. **Adaptation:** Change is inevitable. Success goes to those who recognize when to innovate, when to consolidate, and when to retreat. Machiavelli writes that "one who, wishing to keep his footing, should not stand on all fours, should shift his rear such as to be always prepared to stand straight."

3. **Perception:** Reputation can be as powerful as raw resources. Machiavelli insists that the appearance of virtue—of generosity, mercy, or courage—can sometimes be more effective than the things themselves. Entrepreneurs, too, must manage brand, narrative, and stakeholder expectations to sustain momentum and deter competitors.

How to Use This Book

Structure, Pacing, and Exercises

This book is organized into three parts—Foundations of Entrepreneurial Power, Instruments of Influence, and Sustaining and Scaling the Empire—each mirroring the progression from establishing authority to wielding influence and ultimately ensuring longevity. Within each chapter, you'll find actionable frameworks, real-world case studies, and reflective exercises designed to translate theory into practice. Sidebars prompt you to map your own territory, draft negotiation scripts, or assess your organization's agility, ensuring you don't merely read lessons but apply them.

Navigating from Theory to Actionable Steps
 We begin each chapter by distilling Machiavelli's original maxims—quoted in full context—then layer on modern interpretations and tactical playbooks. Whether you're determining the optimal balance between central control and team autonomy or deciding when to launch your next product pivot, you'll find clear guidelines and decision-trees that walk you through critical junctures. By the end of each section, you'll have concrete next steps: a prioritized checklist, metrics to track, and questions to challenge your assumptions. This is not a passive text; it's a strategic companion that demands engagement, reflection, and decisive action.

With this foundation in place, you are ready to embark on a journey that fuses the timeless wisdom of Machiavelli with the dynamic world of entrepreneurship. Turn the page, and let the lessons of *The Prince* guide you in building, defending, and expanding your own principality in the marketplace.

Chapter 1: Assembling Your Domain

From the moment a founder conceives an idea, they stand at the threshold of forging a new principality. In Machiavelli's terms, every startup is a nascent state—fragile, untested, yet brimming with potential. Just as a prince must secure territory, marshal resources, and earn the loyalty of his subjects, an entrepreneur must claim a market, assemble a team, and establish the values and structures that will sustain growth. In this chapter, we explore the parallels between principalities and startups, define how to map out your entrepreneurial domain, and lay the vital groundwork—mission, vision, values, and initial investments—that will transform a fledgling venture into a flourishing enterprise.

The Parallels between Principalities and Startups

Machiavelli begins *The Prince* by distinguishing different types of principalities—new, hereditary, mixed—and the unique challenges each presents. Similarly, startups can be fresh endeavors entering virgin markets, spin-outs from existing organizations, or ventures branching into adjacent spaces. In all cases, founders face the essential question: how to establish authority, win commitment, and defend the realm against rivals.

When Machiavelli describes a new prince's task of "constructing a city from level ground," he captures the raw opportunity and inherent risks of uncharted territory: without existing structures or loyalties, every decision carries disproportionate weight. For a startup, "level ground" is a market with no entrenched incumbents but also no established demand patterns. The founder's first task is to sculpt that market's contours—to educate potential customers, shape their expectations, and demonstrate why this new offering matters.

Yet even a new prince often inherits a patchwork of unsettled loyalties and rival claimants. Machiavelli warns that these "new states are more difficult to govern than hereditary ones," because they lack the comfort of tradition. Startups, too, must navigate skepticism: investors wary of unproven teams, customers accustomed to legacy solutions, regulators suspicious of novel business models. Overcoming this challenge requires not just a great product but a compelling narrative that binds stakeholders to the venture's success.

Contrast this with hereditary principalities, where a ruler inherits established structures—albeit sometimes ossified ones. Likewise, corporate spin-outs or founder-led expansions benefit from brand recognition, distribution channels, and institutional knowledge. But they face a different peril: complacency and internal resistance. Machiavelli notes that "men change princes not because of the goodness of the new but because of the resentment toward the old," reminding us that when an established organization launches a startup arm, it must guard against the inertia and politics that can sap entrepreneurial energy.

In both politics and business, the size of the principality—or market—matters. Machiavelli observes that "a large dominion is difficult to hold," as it amplifies the complexity of governance and the risk of rebellion. For entrepreneurs, rapid expansion into multiple geographies or verticals can stretch resources thin and dilute focus. The wiser course is often to secure a defensible niche—what Machiavelli would call a naturally fortified region—then extend outward methodically, building on each hard-won stronghold.

Above all, Machiavelli teaches that authority is neither static nor guaranteed. "It is better to be feared than loved," he declares, "if you cannot be both." Translated to entrepreneurship, this means the founder must command respect—through clear standards, decisive leadership, and an unwavering commitment to the venture's values—even as they cultivate goodwill among customers, employees, and partners. A principality built on fickle affection will crumble the moment trials arise; one grounded in earned respect and robust structures can weather storms that would destroy lesser realms.

Defining Your "Territory": Market, Niche, Audience

Before any grand strategy can unfold, an entrepreneur must draw the boundaries of their domain. Unlike medieval lords who claimed physical land, founders stake out intellectual, digital, or service-based territories. These might be defined by:

- **Market sector**: fintech, health tech, edtech, consumer goods, or any other industry vertical.

- **Functional niche**: peer-to-peer lending, remote collaboration tools, personalized nutrition, micro-learning modules.

- **Audience segment**: small businesses, enterprise clients, tech-savvy millennials, underserved rural populations, or other demographic and psychographic clusters.

Machiavelli's advice to princes was blunt: "A wise prince should rely on himself." In entrepreneurial terms, this means choosing a territory where your team's expertise, resources, and network give you a comparative edge. If your founders know embedded systems and have deep ties to aerospace suppliers, launching a B2B drone-analytics platform could be smarter than chasing a crowded consumer-app market.

Moreover, a narrowly defined niche offers natural defenses against rivals. When a prince fortifies mountain passes or rivers, he uses the landscape to deter attackers; so too can a startup use specialization—deep domain knowledge, tailored features, or unique cultural resonance—to erect barriers to entry. Once you dominate your niche, you can leverage that strongpoint as a springboard into adjacent markets or broader segments.

To map your territory:

1. **Assess unmet needs**: Conduct interviews, surveys, and observational research to uncover customer pain points that incumbents ignore or dismiss.

2. **Analyze competitive terrain**: Identify direct competitors (firms solving the same problem), indirect competitors (alternative solutions), and potential entrants (firms with

adjacent offerings).

3. **Define a defensible position**: Articulate how your product
    or service creates unique value—be it through cost
    advantage, superior experience, or proprietary technology.

4. **Segment and prioritize**: Choose the sub-segment where
    you can move fastest and establish a stronghold, rather
    than spreading resources across a diffuse audience.

Machiavelli's counsel on new dominions applies here: "Those who
have relied on their own strength have always overcome those
who have placed their faith in others." By staking out a territory
you truly understand, you can rely on rigorous insight and direct
control rather than hope for serendipitous adoption.

Laying the Groundwork: Mission, Vision, and Values

With territory defined, the next imperative is to articulate the
ideological and operational foundations of your principality.
Machiavelli writes that a prince's reputation hinges on perceived
virtues—generosity, courage, integrity—even if he must
sometimes act contrary to them. For entrepreneurs, mission,
vision, and values serve as the publicly proclaimed virtues that
shape culture, guide decisions, and attract allies.

- **Mission** answers: Why do we exist today? It frames the
  urgent purpose that unites the team and motivates early

adopters.

- **Vision** projects: Where are we heading tomorrow? It stretches the collective imagination, rallying resources toward ambitious, long-term objectives.

- **Values** define: How will we behave along the way? They set the ethical and cultural guardrails that ensure consistency, build trust, and forestall missteps.

When drafting these, resist the temptation to settle for platitudes. Machiavelli admonished princes against empty ceremony: "Men are so simple and so much creatures of circumstance that the deceiver will always find someone ready to be deceived." In entrepreneurial language, hollow mission statements or generic values ring false, erode morale, and fail to distinguish you from the dozens of startups parroting similarly canned ideals.

Instead, infuse your groundwork with specificity and narrative:

1. **Mission rooted in story**: Ground your mission in the founder's journey or in vivid customer scenarios. Rather than "We empower small businesses," consider "We give rural artisans the tools to reach global marketplaces with the click of a button," painting a clear picture of impact.

2. **Vision anchored in possibilities**: Project tangible future states. Instead of "We aim to be industry leaders," articulate "By 2030, every educator in underfunded schools will use our platform to personalize learning paths for their

students."

3. **Values forged from lived experience**: Elicit values from how you've handled real challenges. If your team overcame a crisis through radical transparency, codify "Relentless candor" as a core value, with examples of what candor looks like in action.

This framework does more than inspire; it becomes a strategic compass. When Machiavelli advises that a prince must appear merciful, trustworthy, and pious—even if he must sometimes conceal cruelty—he underscores the power of clear, consistent image. Your mission, vision, and values communicate to customers, investors, and employees what you stand for and what they can expect, cementing loyalty and deterring those who do not align with your purpose.

Early Investments in People and Infrastructure

A principality's strength lies in its armies and fortresses; a startup's in its people and systems. Machiavelli emphasizes the importance of a prince maintaining his own troops rather than relying on mercenaries or auxiliaries, for "mercenaries… have no loyalty; they are dangerous and cowardly." In the entrepreneurial realm, outsourcing your core capabilities or neglecting your internal culture in favor of cheap contractors can spell disaster when your business faces its first real test.

1. Building Your Core Team

The founders and early hires are the startup's nobility and commanders. These individuals carry disproportionate influence in shaping culture, defining standards, and executing strategy.

- **Founders** must wear multiple hats—vision-casting, fundraising, product development—but also know when to delegate. Recruit co-founders whose skills complement yours: if you're a technical visionary, partner with a leader fluent in operations or sales.

- **Early employees** should embody the mission and values, equipped to iterate quickly and comfortable with ambiguity. Machiavelli lauds princes who surround themselves with advisers but retain ultimate decision-making power. In practice, build a small circle of "A-players," trust them with autonomy, yet ensure clear accountability to you and to each other.

- **Advisers and mentors** serve as the prince's counselors. Seek individuals who have weathered downturns, scaled companies, or navigated complex regulations. Their hard-won lessons can preempt missteps that cost precious time and capital.

2. Establishing Operational Systems

A fortress is only as strong as its walls; a startup is only as resilient as its processes. Early investments in infrastructure prevent chaos as you grow.

- **Technology stack**: Choose tools that balance flexibility with reliability. A monolithic codebase may hamper speed, but a sprawling microservices architecture can bog down a small team. Opt for modular, well-supported platforms that allow incremental upgrades—much as a prince reinforces key walls while leaving less critical battlements for later repair.

- **Data and analytics**: Even at earliest stages, instrument your product to capture user behavior. Machiavelli stresses the value of intelligence: "Knowing the disposition of the troops, and the condition of affairs, are there to be attended to first." In startup terms, customer usage data, funnel metrics, and feedback loops become the raw material for informed pivots and feature investments.

- **Financial controls**: Run lean, but not at the expense of visibility. Implement simple budgeting and forecasting models. A surprising number of founders overlook basic bookkeeping until the fiscal stress of a rainy season exposes their lack of reserves—an avoidable crisis that older leaders would have foreseen.

- **Communication protocols**: Define how the team shares updates, raises obstacles, and celebrates wins. Whether through daily stand-ups, weekly all-hands, or collaborative digital workspaces, clear communication is the mortar that holds your organizational bricks together. When Machiavelli describes the prince's need to maintain constant contact with loyal followers, he anticipates this modern imperative: engaged teams are effective teams.

3. Cultivating Loyalty and Motivation

A prince must sometimes bind his subjects with incentives and sometimes with fear. For founders, the equivalent is a mix of cultural motivators and tangible rewards.

- **Equity and incentives**: Early employees often accept lower cash compensation in exchange for equity. Structure vesting schedules that reward longevity and performance, ensuring that those who build the fortress walls also share in the spoils of growth.

- **Culture-building rituals**: Shared experiences—hackathons, offsites, weekly demos—forge bonds and reinforce purpose. Machiavelli recognized the power of pageantry and ritual in unifying subjects; in startups, traditions like all-hands MVP showcases or quarterly learning days serve a similar function, reminding everyone of their collective journey.

- **Feedback and growth**: Establish regular performance conversations, mentorship programs, and skill-development resources. A principality flourishes when its citizens feel their needs are heard and their talents cultivated; a startup thrives when its people perceive a path to greater impact and mastery.

Conclusion of Chapter 1

Assembling your domain is the crucible in which a venture's destiny is forged. By recognizing the profound parallels between Machiavelli's principalities and modern startups, you ground your approach in time-tested strategy. Defining your territory with laser focus, articulating mission, vision, and values with authenticity, and investing early in people and infrastructure lay the unshakable foundation upon which every future achievement depends. In the next chapter, we turn from creation to consolidation—exploring how to secure legitimacy and cultivate the loyalty that transforms a fledgling domain into a resilient principality.

Chapter 2: Securing Legitimacy

In the crucible of Renaissance politics, legitimacy was the currency of power. A prince could command armies, forge alliances, and erect fortifications, but without the consent—either tacit or enthusiastic—of his subjects, his rule would always be precarious. For entrepreneurs, legitimacy is equally vital. It is the foundation upon which customers choose to buy, investors decide to back, and partners commit to collaborate. In this chapter, we explore the sources of entrepreneurial legitimacy—tradition, innovation, and expertise—and examine how to build credibility through thought leadership and social proof. We then unpack the art of balancing authenticity with strategic image management, and conclude with a case study that brings these principles to life.

Sources of Legitimacy: Tradition, Innovation, Expertise

Machiavelli recognized that different princes derive their authority from different wells. Some inherit long-established dynasties; others rise by dint of conquest or shrewd alliances. He writes, "He who becomes prince through the favor of the people ought to keep them friendly by not devoting himself to any of their harms" —a warning that legitimacy grounded in popular support can wither if the ruler betrays the values or expectations of the populace. For entrepreneurs, legitimacy often springs from three main sources: the strength of tradition, the promise of innovation, and the claim of expertise.

Tradition

In Machiavelli's world, hereditary princes benefit from centuries of ritual, ceremony, and custom. Their subjects obey because they have always done so; institutions and norms align in favor of the ruler's continuity. In business, tradition translates into brand heritage and incumbency. Legacy firms like Ford or Procter & Gamble enjoy deep reservoirs of trust cultivated over decades. Even younger companies can evoke a sense of tradition by aligning with enduring values—family, quality craftsmanship, or time-tested methods.

For a startup, invoking tradition can bolster legitimacy when entering markets where consumers seek reassurance. A food brand built around "the grandmother's recipe" narrative or a fintech startup that partners with centuries-old banks leverages tradition as a signal of reliability. But Machiavelli cautions that tradition alone is insufficient: "Men change prince not by the goodness of the new, but by the resentment towards the old." In entrepreneurial terms, clinging to tradition without evolving risks obsolescence; customers may respect your heritage but seek fresher solutions when the status quo grows stale.

Innovation

If tradition undergirds legitimacy for established houses, innovation is the lifeblood of new ones. Machiavelli observed that new princes face greater challenges precisely because they lack inherited structures. Yet he also admired those who could remake the world to their design, writing of Cesare Borgia that he "reoccupied the Romagna swiftly and with little difficulty, for he had [...] the spirit of enterprise." For entrepreneurs, innovation is that spirit of enterprise—reshaping markets, redefining user expectations, and sparking new demand.

When a startup introduces a breakthrough technology or business model, it can bypass legacy competitors and win legitimacy as a pioneer. But innovation's legitimacy is fragile: early adopters may celebrate novelty, but mainstream markets often demand proof of stability, support, and ongoing improvement. A founder must therefore shepherd innovation through the gauntlet of skepticism, providing clear roadmaps for product evolution, demonstrating consistent delivery, and anchoring each new feature in concrete benefits. As Machiavelli advises, a prince must show perseverance in his new institutions: "For those who do not believe in renewing states until the old is worn out […] do not deal with new matters understandingly." Entrepreneurs, too, must be tireless in evolving their innovations, lest customers conclude that the promise of "new" was merely a one-time spectacle.

Expertise

Expertise confers legitimacy by signaling that the founder or team possesses privileged knowledge or capabilities. Machiavelli extols princes who understand the art of war; without military expertise, even the most opulent court would crumble under siege. In the startup realm, domain expertise can be equally vital. A biotech company led by scientists with deep research pedigrees or an AI venture helmed by published experts commands attention and respect that a generalist team may struggle to earn.

Yet expertise must translate into tangible value. Machiavelli warns against "the lion who knows not how to avoid traps" despite his fearsome reputation. Founders must show that their technical

prowess solves real problems at scale, that their algorithms
perform reliably under diverse conditions, and that their patents or
research partnerships truly differentiate them. Sharing white
papers, presenting at conferences, and publishing independent
benchmarks can all cement the perception that you are not merely
dabbling, but are a leader in your field.

Building Credibility: Thought Leadership and Social Proof

Once the sources of legitimacy are identified, the next step is to
amplify them through outward signals. Machiavelli stressed the
power of appearance: "For men judge generally more by the eye
than by the hand." In modern business, two of the most potent
signals are thought leadership and social proof.

Thought Leadership

Thought leadership is the deliberate cultivation of visibility and
authority in a given domain. By consistently sharing insights,
frameworks, and projections, founders can position themselves as
the natural point of reference for prospects, partners, and press.

1. **Content Platforms**
   Writing long-form essays, white papers, and blog posts
   allows founders to unpack complex ideas and demonstrate
   depth. When Machiavelli authored *The Prince*, he was
   essentially publishing a guidebook on realpolitik. Today's
   entrepreneurs can emulate that by releasing
   comprehensive analyses of market trends, playbooks for

emerging challenges, or conceptual models that fellow practitioners adopt.

2. **Speaking Engagements**
   Podcasts, webinars, and conference keynotes put founders in front of live audiences. The ability to articulate vision with clarity and passion cements perceptions of mastery. Machiavelli observed that a prince "must...present himself as compassionate, faithful, humane, upright, and religious," understanding that these traits are partly performed for public consumption. For founders, the stage is the modern court—how you present yourself, the language you use, and the stories you tell become part of your brand's reputation.

3. **Academic and Industry Contributions**
   Collaborating on peer-reviewed journals, sponsoring research, or participating in standards bodies embeds the startup within the fabric of its industry. When competitors cite your work, your legitimacy becomes woven into the broader narrative of what constitutes best practice.

Social Proof

Social proof leverages the behaviors and endorsements of others to signal credibility. Machiavelli understood that princes benefited when notable figures favored them; a cardinal's blessing or a respected noble's loyalty could sway the opinions of thousands.

1. **Customer Testimonials and Case Studies**
   Prospective buyers are reassured when they see peers

successfully using your product. Detailed case studies—complete with metrics on cost savings, revenue growth, or efficiency gains—serve as vignettes of legitimacy. A prince would parade captured banners; a startup parades customer logos and success stories.

2. **Influencer and Media Endorsements**
   Coverage in respected outlets or praise from industry influencers amplifies your standing. Machiavelli noted that, at court, "a prince is esteemed according to the reputation of those who are around him." In business, those "around him" include journalists, analysts, and social media thought leaders whose imprimatur can open doors to new markets.

3. **Partnerships and Alliances**
   Strategic alliances with established firms confer a halo effect. Just as a young prince might marry into a powerful dynasty to cement his position, a startup that announces a pilot with a Fortune 500 or an integration with a dominant platform gains legitimacy by association.

Balancing Authenticity with Strategic Image Management

Machiavelli is often caricatured as the champion of deceit, but a closer reading reveals his insistence that image and reality must cohere when it matters most. He instructs princes to "appear to be merciful, faithful, humane, upright, and religious," cautioning that if a ruler's actions starkly contradict his projected virtues, he will be despised rather than feared.

In entrepreneurship, authenticity is the currency of trust. Customers and employees can often detect hollow posturing, and when they do, the backlash can be swift. Yet a purely laissez-faire approach to brand—eschewing any conscious image management—risks inconsistency and confusion. The art lies in aligning your genuine values and behaviors with the signals you broadcast.

1. **Consistency in Voice and Action**
   If your brand promises transparency, ensure that communication—be it pricing structures, product roadmaps, or corporate governance—is consistently open. When Machiavelli praises the ideal of a ruler who keeps promises only when expedient, he does not excuse capriciousness; he highlights that when deception is necessary, it must be surgical, not wholesale.

2. **Selective Disclosure**
   Entrepreneurs must strike a balance between showcasing strengths and admitting vulnerabilities. A startup raising funds might highlight traction metrics while acknowledging the roadmap ahead. Machiavelli counsels that "a prudent ruler never occupies himself entirely with either affairs: he devotes part of his attention to them both." Similarly, a founder should neither boast relentlessly nor wallow in self-doubt.

3. **Responsive Image Repair**
   No venture is immune from missteps—product failures,

leadership gaffes, regulatory stumbles. When crises strike, the instinct to retreat into silence can worsen perceptions. Machiavelli admired rulers who, when accused unjustly, responded swiftly and strategically; he writes that "injury should be done all at once, so that it does not have time to be ruminated upon; benefits ought to be given little by little, so that they may be tasted and enjoyed every day." Applied to reputation management, this means addressing faults quickly and transparently, then reinforcing your strengths over time so that public memory of the failure fades in light of consistent excellence.

Case Study: A Startup's Journey to Market Credibility

To illustrate these principles in action, consider the hypothetical journey of ClearWave, a healthtech startup aiming to bring AI-driven diagnostics to rural clinics.

Initial Legitimacy via Expertise
ClearWave's founders were leading researchers at a top university's medical school. From day one, they published a white paper in a respected journal detailing their algorithm's performance on historical patient data. This academic pedigree conferred immediate expertise-based legitimacy.

Leveraging Innovation to Carve Territory
Operating in regions ignored by larger diagnostic firms, ClearWave framed its mission around serving underserved

communities—a narrative rooted in social purpose rather than mere profit. By emphasizing innovation in portable, battery-powered devices tuned for low-bandwidth settings, they distinguished themselves from incumbents and attracted early pilot partners in five rural districts.

Building Tradition through Partnership
To invoke the power of tradition, ClearWave struck a partnership with a century-old nonprofit medical association that trained community health workers. Co-branded training programs and shared certification granted ClearWave a veneer of heritage: although a new company, it now appeared part of a longer lineage of trusted health providers.

Thought Leadership and Social Proof
Founders launched a blog series dissecting case studies from the field—how early detection of diabetic retinopathy prevented vision loss in dozens of patients. They spoke at global health conferences, and the World Health Organization cited their pilot results in a white paper on rural diagnostics. Meanwhile, testimonials from local clinics and video interviews with nurses showed clear endorsements, converting skeptics into believers.

Managing Image and Authenticity
When an initial pilot device malfunctioned due to extreme heat, ClearWave's leadership publicly acknowledged the flaw, deployed firmware fixes, and offered extended support visits at no cost. They shared their learnings in a webinar titled "Designing Resilient MedTech for Tough Climates," turning a crisis into a demonstration of responsiveness and care. Over time, this blend of authenticity and strategic repair bolstered trust far more than if they had simply brushed the incident under the rug.

Outcome: A Defensible Position
 Within two years, ClearWave secured a multi-year procurement contract with the national health ministry. Their mix of expertise, innovative solutions tailored to local needs, partnerships that evoked tradition, and a meticulously managed public image transformed them from an academic research spin-out into the de facto standard for rural diagnostics.

Conclusion

Securing legitimacy is not a one-time campaign but an ongoing strategy. Machiavelli's lessons remind us that the foundations of authority—tradition, innovation, and expertise—must be nurtured, displayed, and occasionally defended. Thought leadership and social proof amplify these sources, while adept image management ensures that authenticity and perception march in lockstep. As demonstrated by ClearWave's journey, the entrepreneurs who master these dynamics command not only market share but the enduring trust of customers, investors, and partners. In the next chapter, we will delve into the art of adaptation—how to pivot, evolve, and stay ahead when the landscape shifts beneath your feet.

Chapter 3: Mastering Adaptation

In the ever-shifting terrain of business, the capacity to adapt is the difference between fleeting success and enduring dominion. Machiavelli observed the fates of princes who either clung rigidly to tradition or embraced change with shrewd timing. His lessons on "new" versus "hereditary" states, on knowing when to pivot, on managing risk in uncharted realms, and on cultivating a mindset—and a culture—of agility offer entrepreneurs a blueprint for navigating uncertainty with confidence and foresight.

Lessons from New vs. Hereditary States

Machiavelli begins his treatise by distinguishing principalities inherited through lineage from those acquired by one's own prowess. He notes that hereditary states "require few changes, for customs, laws, and taxes established by the ancestors give contentment" and thereby ensure stability. In contrast, new principalities—those carved out by conquest or fortune—pose monumental challenges: "When a prince acquires a new state, he will always face difficulties in maintaining it."

Inherited Structures vs. Fresh Foundations
Hereditary states enjoy an advantage akin to a legacy brand: ingrained institutions, established loyalties, and a shared memory of "how things have always been done." Customers know the product, employees understand the culture, and regulators already trust the company's compliance record. But this inheritance can

calcify into inertia. Machiavelli warns that "custom in governance, like habit in men, is long and difficult to change." An entrenched organization may resist innovation, dismissing new ideas as threats rather than opportunities.

New startups, by contrast, build from "level ground," unencumbered by legacy systems but lacking the safety net of tested routines. Machiavelli admired those who, when entering a new state, could swiftly establish order by creating institutions of their own: "He must introduce new modes and orders; and he who introduces them must build according to his own vision." For entrepreneurs, this means designing processes, structures, and cultural norms from the outset—modeling them not on what incumbents do, but on what best aligns with the venture's unique mission and operational realities.

Strategies for Hereditary Entities

- **Identify and Dismantle Deadwood:** Conduct honest audits of existing practices. Which legacy systems hinder speed or innovation? Which policies no longer serve customers' needs?

- **Introduce Incremental Change:** Instead of wholesale overhauls that trigger organizational trauma, roll out pilot programs. Test a new customer-centric workflow in one division before scaling.

- **Leverage Institutional Memory:** Use the brand's heritage as a launchpad for innovation. A storied brand entering a new market can reference its history of quality to reassure early adopters and justify a higher price point.

Strategies for New Entrants

- **Design for Flexibility:** Build modular product architectures and flat communication structures. Just as Machiavelli's ideal prince creates laws that encourage loyalty and adaptability, founders should craft company handbooks and job roles that empower employees to improvise when circumstances demand.

- **Establish Early Rituals:** Forge identity through shared practices—daily stand-ups, customer hackathons, or cohort-based onboarding. These rituals, though novel, become the bedrock of company culture, reducing the perceived risk of joining an untested venture.

- **Sculpt a Clear Narrative:** A new prince must justify his rule; likewise, a startup must articulate why it exists. This origin story becomes a rallying cry, attracting talent, investors, and customers who identify with the mission's urgency.

By understanding these distinctions, entrepreneurs can tailor their approach to adaptation. Hereditary incumbents must fight the gravitational pull of the status quo, while new ventures must move swiftly to codify their own governing principles before chaos takes hold.

Rapid Pivots: Knowing When and How to Change Course

One of Machiavelli's core insights is that the political landscape is never static: alliances shift, rivalries flare, and "fortune is the arbiter of half our actions." Today's entrepreneurs face analogous dynamics: a regulatory change can render a business model obsolete overnight; a competitor's breakthrough can shift customer expectations; a global event can disrupt entire supply chains. Mastery of adaptation demands not only the willingness to pivot but the wisdom to know precisely when and how.

Signals for a Pivot

1. **Consistent Underdelivery on Key Metrics:** If customer acquisition costs keep rising despite optimization efforts, or if retention rates plateau even after product improvements, it may signal that the current value proposition misses the mark.

2. **Market Feedback That Contradicts Core Assumptions:** When face-to-face interviews, surveys, and usage data reveal that customers value aspects of the product you never prioritized, you must consider reorienting development.

3. **Technological Disruption or Regulatory Shifts:** A sudden regulatory clarification can open new markets or close off existing ones. Similarly, the emergence of a complementary technology (e.g., blockchain, 5G, AI) can

necessitate a strategic rethink.

Machiavelli counsels that a prince must be "like the fox and the lion: the lion to scare wolves, the fox to recognize traps." In business, the lion represents decisive action—a bold reallocation of resources or a public strategic announcement—while the fox represents due diligence, scanning for hidden risks and opportunities.

Framework for a Disciplined Pivot

- **Rapid Experimentation:** Emulate the Prince's agile campaigns. Before redirecting the entire company, launch small, controlled tests: a minimum-viable feature, a marketing pilot in a new segment, or a prototype partnership.

- **Cross-Functional Steering Committees:** Bring together product, marketing, finance, and customer success to interpret data holistically. Machiavelli emphasized the value of diverse counsel; today's pivots benefit from multiple expert perspectives to avoid blind spots.

- **Transparent Stakeholder Communication:** Just as Machiavelli's ideal ruler "does not conceal his intentions," a founder must articulate the rationale for the pivot to employees, investors, and customers—balancing honesty about the need for change with confidence in the new direction.

- **Iterative Review Cadence:** Establish a weekly or biweekly "pivot review" where teams assess progress, share learnings, and decide whether to double down, tweak, or abandon the new initiative.

Case in Point

Consider a SaaS startup originally built around small-business bookkeeping. After months of modest traction and overwhelming feedback that customers valued its automated tax-prep features above all else, the company shifted focus: it spun off bookkeeping into an optional add-on and rebranded as a tax optimization platform. By treating the pivot as a series of experiments—landing page A/B tests, targeted ads to accountants, early adopter incentives—they validated the new model before sunsetting legacy features. Revenues then accelerated tenfold within six months, demonstrating the power of rapid, data-informed course corrections.

Risk Management in Uncharted Markets

When Machiavelli's prince entered a newly conquered territory, he faced unknown loyalties, unfamiliar customs, and the constant threat of rebellion. He advised: "First, he must examine whether to keep the ancient tax and the ancient laws or to introduce new ones." Neither choice guarantees safety; the prudent prince weighs potential benefits against the dangers of alienating the populace.

Entrepreneurs venturing into emerging industries—cryptocurrency, synthetic biology, decentralized finance—encounter parallel uncertainties. No historical benchmark provides a roadmap, and conventional risk-mitigation tools may not apply. Effective risk management in these contexts requires creativity, vigilance, and a bias toward optionality.

Layers of Risk in New Markets

1. **Regulatory Risk:** Ambiguous or evolving regulations can criminalize business models overnight.

2. **Technology Risk:** Immature technologies may lack stability or scalability.

3. **Market Adoption Risk:** Customer behavior may not conform to theoretical projections.

4. **Operational Risk:** Supply chains, talent pools, or support ecosystems may be underdeveloped.

Adaptive Risk-Mitigation Strategies

- **Staged Market Entry:** Rather than launching nationwide or globally, select a single jurisdiction with favorable regulation or a friendlier investor ecosystem. Use this "sandbox" to learn and optimize before expanding.

- **Regulator Engagement:** Proactively engage with policymakers and industry groups. Machiavelli valued commanders who understood local terrain; entrepreneurs must cultivate relationships with regulators, participate in public comment periods, and help shape emerging standards.

- **Flexible Legal Structures:** Employ special purpose vehicles, partnerships, or joint ventures that can be restructured quickly if regulations tighten—much like a prince might appoint regional governors with limited tenure to prevent any one official from amassing too much power.

- **Robust Scenario Planning:** Develop a spectrum of "what-if" scenarios—from best case to worst case—and assign clear trigger points. If exchange volumes drop below a certain threshold, pivot marketing spend; if a critical component's price spikes by more than 20%, switch to an alternative supplier.

Embedding Optionality

Machiavelli applauds rulers who maintain multiple lines of retreat: "A prince must always think of a means by which he may turn and fight another day." Entrepreneurs can mirror this by avoiding "all-in" bets. Instead of allocating the entire R&D budget to a single prototype, split resources across complementary experiments. If one fails, others may still succeed, and the organization preserves the capacity to pursue new avenues.

Developing an Organizational Culture of Agility

Adaptation is not merely a series of tactical moves; it is a mindset that must permeate the organization. Machiavelli reminds us that "there is nothing more difficult to carry out…than to initiate a new order of things." The resistance to change resides not in external forces alone, but in human nature—fear of the unknown, comfort with routine, and the inertia of past successes.

Principles for an Agile Culture

1. **Embrace Learning over Perfection:** Treat failures as experiments that yield insight. Incentivize teams to share "lessons learned" openly, without fear of blame. Machiavelli counsels that princes who punish honest mistakes stifle initiative and breed hypocrisy.

2. **Decentralize Decision-Making:** Push authority to the edges. Just as a prince cannot oversee every minor indiscipline, a founder cannot vet every small decision. Empower small, cross-functional squads to own outcomes, accelerating response times.

3. **Visible Metrics and Accountability:** Publish key performance indicators on public dashboards. Transparency drives focus and fosters collective responsibility—when everyone sees the customer-churn rate ticking up, they coalesce around solutions.

4. **Continuous Feedback Loops:** Install mechanisms for rapid feedback from customers, partners, and frontline employees. Machiavelli admired spies and informants who kept princes apprised of sentiment; in startups, customer success teams, community forums, and direct-from-the-user data serve that role.

5. **Adaptive Leadership Rituals:** Schedule "pivot retrospectives" alongside standard sprint reviews. Ask: What new information has emerged? What norms no longer serve us? Which experiments should we launch next? These rituals normalize change as a constant rather than an emergency.

Overcoming Cultural Barriers

- **Resistance to Change:** Early on, recruit "change champions"—individuals who naturally enjoy problem-solving and experimentation. Their enthusiasm can inoculate others against fear of novelty.

- **Siloed Teams:** Break down functional walls by organizing squads around customer journeys rather than departmental specialties. When product, design, and engineering share a mission to improve a specific metric, they learn to adapt together.

- **Information Hoarding:** Combat knowledge silos by documenting decisions in shared repositories and rotating team members through different roles or projects. This cross-pollination builds collective fluency in both strategy and execution.

Sustaining Agility at Scale

As the organization grows, the informal structures that once enabled rapid adaptation can ossify into process overhead. Machiavelli noted that large principalities require different tactics than small ones; similarly, startups must evolve their agile practices:

- **Scaled Agile Frameworks:** Adopt lightweight scaling methods that preserve small-team autonomy—two-pizza squads, tribe-and-guild systems, or networked micro-enterprises within the larger company.

- **Leadership Alignment:** Ensure that executives model the behaviors they expect from frontline teams: quick decision-making, openness to new data, and the humility to reverse course when necessary.

- **Cultural Gatekeepers:** Appoint internal champions—"Chief Adaptability Officers" or "Innovation Sherpas"—tasked with monitoring rigidities, surfacing broken processes, and mentoring teams in agile practices.

Conclusion of Chapter 3

Machiavelli's teachings on adaptation transcend the battlefields and courts of Renaissance Italy; they speak to the heart of entrepreneurial survival. Whether navigating the relative safety of a hereditary organization or the turbulence of a nascent startup, founders must learn to balance the gravitational pull of tradition with the imperative of innovation. They must cultivate the fox's cunning and the lion's resolve, pivot swiftly when conditions change, and manage risks in unknown territories with both caution and courage. Above all, they must embed agility into their organizational DNA—crafting cultures where learning is prized, authority is distributed, and change is not feared but embraced as the lifeblood of lasting success. In the next chapter, we will turn to the art of alliances and coalitions: forging partnerships that extend your reach, amplify your strengths, and fortify your principality against the inevitable storms to come.

Chapter 4: The Art of Alliances

In the volatile world of Renaissance principalities, no prince reigned entirely alone. Alliances—shifting, fragile, yet potentially decisive—shaped the balance of power across Italy's patchwork of states. Machiavelli understood that alliances could fortify a ruler's position or become the very chains that led to his downfall. "He who relies entirely on auxiliaries, places his own life and that of his state in the hands of another," he warned. For entrepreneurs navigating today's fast-moving markets, partnerships, joint ventures, and networks serve a similar dual role: when managed astutely, they expand reach, share risk, and accelerate growth; when misjudged, they breed over-dependence, dilute control, and expose the venture to external shocks. In this chapter, we explore the art of coalition-building, the craft of negotiating agreements that align with long-term strategy, the imperative of avoiding reliance on any single partner, and the tactical wisdom of retreat and realignment when alliances falter.

Coalition-Building: Partnerships, Joint Ventures, and Networks

Just as Machiavelli's princes sought pacts with neighboring states and powerful families, modern entrepreneurs pursue alliances to combine resources, enter new markets, and co-create value. But alliance-building is not mere matchmaking; it demands a strategic framework that assesses potential partners' capabilities, incentives, and cultural fit.

Identifying Complementary Strengths

Machiavelli observed that alliances are strongest when each party brings indispensable resources. He praised Francesco Sforza for leveraging his military prowess and forging marriage ties with leading families—thus combining martial strength with dynastic legitimacy. Similarly, entrepreneurs must map their own strengths—technology, market access, brand reputation—and seek partners whose assets fill critical gaps.

Begin by conducting a **capabilities audit**: list your firm's core competencies (proprietary technology, customer base, distribution channels, regulatory expertise) alongside your weaknesses (limited capital, narrow geographic reach, early-stage brand). Then identify potential allies—suppliers, distributors, complementary-service providers, or even nonprofit organizations—whose strengths correspond to your weaknesses. A healthtech startup might partner with an established medical device manufacturer to gain regulatory know-how; a fintech firm might ally with community banks to tap into existing deposit bases and compliance frameworks.

Structuring Joint Ventures for Shared Value

Joint ventures represent a deeper form of coalition, in which two or more entities commit resources to a co-owned enterprise. Machiavelli admired those princes who "introduce new modes and orders" by creating institutions of their own design. A well-structured joint venture can serve as precisely such an institution: a bespoke vehicle with governance mechanisms tailored to the alliance's goals.

Key elements of joint-venture design include:

1. **Equity Contribution and Control Rights:** Determine each partner's capital, IP, personnel, and facility contributions, and align ownership percentages accordingly. Grant veto rights or board seats on decisions that touch a partner's core interests.

2. **Governance Mechanisms:** Establish a joint steering committee with clear decision thresholds—unanimity for strategic shifts, qualified majority for operational changes. Machiavelli stressed the importance of counsel: "A prince ought to choose wise men… that they may advise him." In a joint venture, that counsel must come from both sides equitably.

3. **Performance Metrics and Incentives:** Define KPIs—revenue targets, margin thresholds, market share goals—and link partner returns to performance. Where feasible, include clawback provisions if one party fails to deliver agreed resources.

4. **Exit and Dissolution Protocols:** Anticipate the endgame. Whether the venture matures, underperforms, or external conditions change, partners must have clear, agreed-upon paths to exit: buy-sell mechanisms, put/call options, or pre-defined auction processes.

By constructing joint ventures with precision, entrepreneurs can capture the benefits of scale and shared risk without surrendering strategic autonomy.

Cultivating Informal Networks

Beyond formal partnerships, Machiavelli recognized the potency of informal alliances—personal bonds, patronage ties, and intelligence networks that operated beneath official treaties. For founders, cultivating such networks means building a web of relationships that provide market insight, talent referrals, and early-warning signals of competitive moves.

1. **Industry Circles and Consortia:** Join trade associations, standard-setting bodies, and innovation hubs. Active participation—speaking at events, serving on committees—yields credibility and access to the "inner circle" of decision-makers.

2. **Advisory Councils and Boards:** Invite respected figures—former regulators, veteran CEOs, renowned academics—to advise. These relationships may be unpaid or lightly compensated, but they offer invaluable counsel and confer legitimacy. Machiavelli extolled the value of wise advisors, even while reminding princes that ultimate judgment rests with the ruler himself.

3. **Peer-to-Peer Founder Communities:** Slack groups, mastermind forums, and accelerator cohorts provide confidential venues for exchanging strategic challenges and solutions. In Machiavelli's day, a prince's spies kept him informed of court intrigues; today, your network can reveal funding shifts, hiring booms, or emerging regulatory concerns well before they hit the headlines.

By layering formal partnerships with robust informal networks, entrepreneurs create a resilience that no individual alliance alone can provide.

Negotiating Agreements that Serve Long-Term Goals

Even the most promising alliance can founder on misaligned incentives or vague terms. Machiavelli counseled princes to secure lasting commitments through clear covenants: "Promises made through force must be kept because men are less apprehensive of injury from one who is loved than from one who is feared." In startup-land, force may be replaced by contractual deterrents—liquidated damages, exclusivity clauses, or equity vesting triggers—but the principle remains: agreements must bind partners in ways that endure beyond initial goodwill.

Anchoring Negotiations in Mutual Benefit

Effective negotiation begins with a joint value-creation mindset: each side must see that the alliance generates more value together than separately. Prepare by:

- **Developing a Shared Value Map:** Articulate explicitly how each partner gains—cost reductions, revenue enhancements, new customer segments—and quantify these where possible.

- **Understanding BATNAs (Best Alternatives to a Negotiated Agreement):** Assess your fallback options if the alliance fails. This gives you leverage and helps calibrate which terms to fight for and where to compromise.

- **Prioritizing Issues:** Rank negotiation points by strategic importance—control rights and IP ownership at the top, non-core operational details lower. This focus prevents dilution of energy and ensures you secure critical protections first.

Drafting Durable Contracts

Contracts are the skeleton on which alliances hang. To avoid ambiguity:

1. **Define Scope and Deliverables in Detail:** Rather than "partner will support marketing efforts," specify campaign types, budgets, target geographies, and reporting formats.

2. **Set Clear Timelines and Milestones:** Incorporate phase-gates—proof of concept, pilot deployment, commercial launch—each tied to decision points on continuing or scaling the venture.

3. **Embed Dispute-Resolution Mechanisms:** Include mediation or arbitration clauses with agreed jurisdictions and procedures to resolve conflicts swiftly and confidentially. Machiavelli would have appreciated this tactic: avoiding protracted legal battles preserves both resources and relationships.

4. **Align Exit Triggers with Performance:** Define objective criteria (revenue below X for two quarters, regulatory changes, key-man departures) that allow one or both parties to exit gracefully, with pre-agreed buyout formulas or equity redemption terms.

By negotiating with an eye toward both opportunity and risk, entrepreneurs craft alliances that endure beyond initial enthusiasm.

Avoiding Over-Dependence on Any Single Partner

Machiavelli's stark admonition still resonates: "Auxiliaries are but borrowed troops and are dangerous; because they are disunited." Dependence on a single partner—whether for distribution, technology, or capital—leaves a startup vulnerable to that partner's shifting priorities. If a dominant ally withdraws support, the startup may find itself defenseless.

Diversification of Dependencies

To safeguard autonomy and resilience:

1. **Layer Multiple Suppliers and Channels:** If your product relies on a critical component, source it from at least two vendors. If distribution runs through a major platform, cultivate alternative channels—direct sales, secondary

marketplaces, white-label arrangements.

2. **Stagger Partnership Maturities:** Structure contracts so that expiration dates are staggered. Rather than all alliances renewing in the same quarter, spread renewal points across the year to avoid simultaneous renegotiation pressure.

3. **Balance Equity and Non-Equity Partnerships:** Equity investments from a strategic partner can bring capital and commitment, but also expectations of control. Mix these with looser alliances—co-marketing agreements, referral programs—to retain options.

Monitoring Partner Health and Intent

Dependence risk is not static. A partner's strategic focus, financial health, or leadership can shift—sometimes abruptly. Maintain vigilance by:

- **Regular Executive Alignment Reviews:** Host quarterly check-ins at the C-suite level to reaffirm goals, surface concerns, and adjust commitments.

- **Joint KPI Dashboards:** Share real-time data on sales, customer satisfaction, and operational metrics. Sudden dips may signal waning partner engagement.

- **Stakeholder Mapping and Influence Analysis:** Periodically update your picture of who holds decision power at the partner organization—new board members, shifted sponsorship, or reorganizations can all alter the alliance dynamic.

By actively diversifying dependencies and monitoring partner health, entrepreneurs inoculate their ventures against the shock of a single ally's retreat.

Tactical Retreats and Re-Alignments

Not every alliance endures. Machiavelli understood that a wise prince, confronted with a disadvantageous pact, must be willing to break it decisively: "When a prince ceases to observe fidelity, promises, and generosity, he must do so in such a way that his subjects cannot forget it." In entrepreneurial terms, pulling back from a failing partnership—or re-aligning strategic priorities—requires both speed and subtlety to preserve reputation and pivot resources effectively.

Recognizing the Need to Retreat

Warning signs that an alliance has turned toxic or unproductive often mirror those that prompt pivots:

- **Persistent Underperformance:** The joint venture fails to meet key milestones despite remedial efforts.

- **Misaligned Incentives:** One party derives outsized benefit while the other bears most costs.

- **Cultural Clash:** Operational frictions, communication breakdowns, or trust erosion impede collaboration.

- **External Changes:** Regulatory shifts, competitive disruptions, or partner reorganizations render the alliance obsolete.

Entrepreneurs must track these signs impartially, resisting the sunk-cost trap that urges "one more quarter" to salvage a flailing partnership.

Executing a Clean Break

When retreat is necessary, Machiavelli urges decisiveness: "In the actions of men, and especially of princes, from which there is no appeal, the ending is always judged a success." A clean break minimizes ambiguity and allows both sides to move forward without lingering resentments.

1. **Invoke Exit Provisions with Clarity:** Rely on the contractual clauses agreed upfront—trigger the buy-sell, enforce the put option, or wind down the joint entity as specified.

2. **Communicate Strategically:** To employees, frame the retreat as a re-allocation of resources toward higher-priority initiatives. To customers, underscore your commitment to service continuity and reveal alternative solutions. To the market, maintain a tone of professionalism, avoiding public finger-pointing that could

damage future alliance prospects.

3. **Reassign Resources Swiftly:** Redeploy personnel from the dissolved partnership to other high-value projects. Capture their experiential learnings in a "partnership postmortem" to inform future alliances.

4. **Preserve Valuable Relationships:** Even as the formal alliance ends, identify individuals within the partner organization with whom productive ties remain. Facilitating their transition—introducing them to other networks or vendors—can maintain goodwill and keep doors open for future collaboration.

Realigning Strategic Focus

Retreating from one alliance is an opportunity to re-express strategic intent. Machiavelli extolled those princes who seized weakening allies or neutralized former partners to strengthen their position. While entrepreneurs should not emulate treachery, they can:

- **Form New Coalitions:** Replace the old partnership with alliances better matched to current objectives—entering new markets, accessing fresh technology, or tapping alternative funding sources.

- **Refocus Core Capabilities:** Channel energy back into proprietary strengths—product innovation, direct sales excellence, or customer success—rather than diluting efforts across misaligned ventures.

- **Reaffirm Vision to Stakeholders:** Use the realignment as a narrative moment: "We are doubling down on X, where we see greatest customer enthusiasm and competitive edge," thus rallying the team and reassuring investors.

Conclusion of Chapter 4

Machiavelli's lessons on alliances are as pertinent to today's entrepreneurs as they were to Renaissance princes. Coalitions—whether formal joint ventures or informal networks—amplify a startup's power, extend its reach, and share the burdens of growth. Yet every alliance carries risk: misalignment of incentives, over-dependence, and the possibility of betrayal. By identifying partners whose strengths complement your own, negotiating agreements that lock in long-term mutual benefit, diversifying dependencies to avoid single-point failures, and executing tactical retreats when necessary, founders wield alliances not as crutches but as strategic force multipliers. In the next chapter, we delve into the communication strategies that transform influence into action—how to craft narratives, manage crises, and command attention in a crowded marketplace.

Chapter 5: Communication as Command

In the swirling currents of Renaissance Italy, reputation and perception were as decisive as armies and fortresses. Machiavelli reminds us that "men judge generally more by the eye than by the hand," and thus the prince who masters the art of perception can wield influence that outstrips his material resources. For entrepreneurs, communication is not a mere support function—it is command itself. The narratives you craft, the channels you deploy, and the tone you strike will determine whether your vision ignites passion or falls flat. In this chapter, we explore how to harness the power of narrative by crafting a founder story that resonates; design public relations, content, and media strategies that amplify your message; balance consistency with the flexibility your evolving venture demands; and, when crisis strikes, remain composed under fire so that every challenge becomes an opportunity to reinforce trust.

The Power of Narrative: Crafting Your Founder Story

Machiavelli opens *The Prince* with clear-eyed realism: power resides not in virtue alone but in the perception of virtue. He counsels that a ruler must "appear to be merciful, faithful, humane, upright, and religious," understanding that these impressions carry more sway than reality to the average subject. In the entrepreneurial realm, your founder story is the vessel through which you project those desired virtues. It is the narrative lens that colors every investor pitch, interview article, and hiring conversation. A compelling founder story turns faceless startups into movements; it transforms customers into believers.

Elements of a Resonant Founder Story

1. **Origin Moment**: Identify the vivid spark that compelled you to act. Machiavelli's own odyssey—from diplomat to exile to political philosopher—arose from a dramatic fall from power. Your origin moment should echo that drama: the customer encounter that seared a problem into your consciousness; the moment of personal frustration so acute it demanded invention; the flash of insight that reframed an industry. A well-told origin moment conveys urgency and authenticity in a single sentence.

2. **Core Conflict**: Every good story pits protagonist against obstacle. What systemic injustice or entrenched flaw did you resolve to confront? Machiavelli admired princes who recognized that "fortune is the ruler of one-half of our actions," but still seized agency where they could. Frame your venture as an act of agency in the face of an indifferent market or recalcitrant incumbents.

3. **Transformation Arc**: Show how you rallied resources, adapted, and grew. Investors and employees alike crave the sense that you not only conceive bold visions but navigate the chaos to realize them. Machiavelli recounts Caesar Borgia's relentless reforms in the Romagna—building bridges, fortifying towns, and winning

hearts—to illustrate the transformative power of decisive action. Your arc should likewise map risk, failure, learning, and triumph.

4. **Values Through Action**: Don't merely list your company's values; demonstrate them through narrative. If "relentless customer empathy" is your north star, share the anecdote of the late-night store call you personally answered, or the weekend you spent redesigning onboarding flows based on user feedback. This echoes Machiavelli's aphorism that "a prince must know how to do wrong," but only when necessity demands—implying that virtues matter most when they require deliberate effort.

5. **Vision Foreshadowing**: Finally, anchor the story in an inspiring future. Just as Machiavelli sketches the ideal republic as a guiding star for princes, your founder story should close with a glimmer of what the world becomes when you succeed. Paint a vivid picture: factories running on your clean energy; teachers reaching every student through your platform; patients initiating telehealth visits in the most remote villages. The vision fuels commitment long after the origin fades from memory.

Storytelling Formats

- **Investor Deck Narrative**: Integrate the founder story into the first few slides so that every subsequent metric and projection resonates as part of a coherent journey.

- **"About Us" Webpage**: Weave prose and multimedia (photos, short video) to create an immersive brand introduction.

- **Keynote Opening**: Begin every major presentation by recounting the origin moment in two minutes or less—personal, emotive, and rooted in your mission.

- **Sales Conversation Hook**: Train your sales team to connect product features to the founder story's conflict and values, ensuring that every demo feels part of the larger narrative.

By consciously architecting and retelling your founder story across channels, you establish a narrative command that orients all stakeholders toward your venture's purpose and potential.

Public Relations, Content Strategy, and Media Relations

Once your narrative is clear, the next task is to amplify it through earned and owned channels. Machiavelli understood that a prince's reputation could be bolstered or besmirched by courtiers, ambassadors, and rival propagandists. For modern founders, the court comprises journalists, bloggers, analysts, and social-media audiences. A disciplined public relations and content strategy ensures that your story reaches sympathetic ears and resonates with strategic impact.

Public Relations: Shaping the External Narrative

1. **Media Mapping**: Catalog outlets—trade publications, tech blogs, business journals, and mainstream press—whose audiences align with your target customers, talent pools, and investors. Assess each outlet's editorial calendar and pitching preferences.

2. **Narrative Angles**: Translate your founder story into multiple compelling hooks: funding announcements, product launches, data-driven reports, customer success milestones, and visionary thought leadership pieces. Machiavelli notes that a prince must "entertain and captivate," and so your PR must blend substance with storytelling flair.

3. **Press Kit Essentials**: Maintain an up-to-date media kit with founder bios, high-resolution images, product screenshots, one-pagers, and a concise FAQ. The easier you make it for reporters to cover you accurately, the more control you retain over the narrative.

4. **Proactive Outreach**: Cultivate relationships with beat reporters and editors. Offer exclusives when you have truly newsworthy developments, and provide expert commentary on broader industry trends. Machiavelli's princes relied on informants and rumor networks; you build networks of trusted journalists who view you as a reliable source.

Content Strategy: Owning Your Domain

Owned content—blogs, newsletters, white papers, podcasts, and video channels—gives you unfiltered access to audiences. Machiavelli would recognize the power of such direct channels to bypass hostile courts and reach subjects directly.

1. **Editorial Calendar**: Plan themes and formats months in advance, tying major content campaigns to product features, industry events, or seasonal trends. Aim for a mix of evergreen cornerstone pieces and timely commentary.

2. **Thought Leadership Pillars**: Base your content on three to five core themes—data privacy, AI ethics, remote work culture, for example—aligned with your company's expertise. By consistently publishing high-quality material in these areas, you become the go-to voice for both prospects and industry peers.

3. **Multi-Format Syndication**: Repurpose long-form articles into slide decks, infographics, podcast episodes, and social-media snippets. This broadens reach and reinforces messages across different consumption preferences.

4. **Measurement and Optimization**: Track engagement metrics—time on page, download rates, social shares, newsletter open rates—and refine your approach based on what drives pipeline and brand lift. Machiavelli valued "knowing the disposition of one's troops"; for founders, knowing your content's performance is equally critical.

Media Relations: Managing Third-Party Visibility

Strategic media coverage lends credibility that owned channels cannot fully replicate. But such coverage also entails risks—misquotation, sensationalism, and fleeting attention. Machiavelli counsels that princes should "appear liberal, but be economical," suggesting a balance between openness and control.

1. **Preparation and Messaging Guides**: Before any interview, arm your spokespeople with key messages, anticipated tough questions, and bridging statements that steer conversations back to your narrative. Role-play challenging scenarios so spokespeople remain composed.

2. **Spokesperson Tiering**: Designate primary and secondary spokespeople—founders for visionary topics, VPs for product deep dives, customer-success leaders for client stories. Ensure each has media training and messaging alignment.

3. **Rapid Response Protocols**: Monitor coverage and social media in real time. Assign a media liaison to flag inaccuracies or emerging issues, and decide when to correct on the record versus when to let minor misstatements lie. Machiavelli recognized that "injury must be done all at once," meaning that swift correction prevents rumor from festering.

4. **Long-Term Relationships**: Treat journalists as allies, not adversaries. Offer them timely data, early access to executives, and background briefings under embargo.

Over time, they will seek your commentary proactively, reducing your need for cold outreach.

Consistency vs. Flexibility in Messaging

A hallmark of Machiavellian strategy is the tension between appearance and expedience. He writes that a prince must "appear to be steadfast in his principles, while in fact adapting to circumstances." Entrepreneurs similarly face the challenge of maintaining a consistent brand voice and core messages even as markets evolve and strategic priorities shift.

The Case for Consistency

- **Trust Building**: Repeating core messages across channels and over time cements recognition and credibility. Just as subjects in Florence learned what to expect from their rulers, customers and partners learn what to expect from your brand.

- **Clarity of Purpose**: A consistent message—around mission, value proposition, and differentiators—prevents confusion. Machiavelli observes that "when a ruler changes the laws and taxes abruptly, subjects become discontent." Sudden shifts in messaging risk alienating audiences.

- **Efficiency in Execution**: Standardized messaging reduces the friction in creating new content or training new spokespeople. It becomes second nature to embed the brand's talking points into every slide deck or press release.

The Case for Flexibility

- **Adaptation to New Contexts**: When regulations change, competitors launch disruptive technologies, or customer priorities realign, messaging must evolve. Machiavelli would approve: "He who adapts to the times succeeds."

- **Audience Segmentation**: Different stakeholders—customers, investors, regulators, employees—respond to tailored messages. A single rigid script may not resonate across cultures, industries, or maturity stages.

- **Crisis and Opportunity**: In moments of crisis or breakthrough, nuanced messaging can mitigate damage or amplify success. As Machiavelli notes, "injury should be done all at once; benefits ought to be given little by little." Timing and framing matter.

Balancing Act: A Framework

1. **Foundational Messaging Platform**: Document your non-negotiable core—company purpose, promise, and personality traits. These anchors never change.

2. **Adaptive Messaging Playbooks**: For key scenarios—fundraising, product launch, crisis response—prepare modular message sets that weave in core elements but shift emphasis as needed.

3. **Governance and Review**: Establish a cross-functional messaging council—marketing, communications, legal, product—charged with vetting significant departures from standard messaging and ensuring alignment with overall strategy.

4. **Regular Message Audits**: Quarterly, review all major public-facing content to ensure that evolving messages remain tethered to foundational principles. Update guides and retrain spokespeople as necessary.

By institutionalizing both the guardrails of consistency and the levers of flexibility, entrepreneurs can navigate changing circumstances without losing narrative coherence.

Crisis Communication: Staying Composed Under Fire

Even the most meticulously planned communication strategy can be upended by crises—product failures, data breaches, regulatory investigations, or leadership scandals. Machiavelli addresses such upheavals directly: "A prince must not mind incurring the charge of cruelty when necessary to keep the state intact." In startup terms, a founder must not shy away from hard truths or decisive action when trust is at stake. The goal in crisis communication is not to spin or obfuscate, but to manage perception through transparency, speed, and empathy.

Principles of Machiavellian Crisis Management

1. **Swift Acknowledgment**: Like a prince who resolves a rebellion by striking quickly, a founder must publicly acknowledge the issue before rumors metastasize. Silence breeds speculation.

2. **Controlled Transparency**: Share what you know honestly. Machiavelli warns against vacillation: "Promises made through force must be kept." In crisis response, keep commitments to investigate, remedy, and communicate clear, achievable next steps.

3. **Decisive Action**: Outline the concrete measures you are taking—security audits, product patches, leadership changes. The public craves evidence that you are not paralyzed.

4. **Empathy and Reassurance**: Address stakeholder fears directly. A prince who consoles displaced subjects can restore loyalty; a founder who acknowledges customer frustration and offers remediation is more likely to regain trust.

Crisis Communication Playbook

1. **Crisis Team Mobilization**

   - Assemble a rapid-response team: communications, legal, engineering, customer success, and HR. Assign clear roles—who drafts external statements, who handles customer support, who fields media inquiries.

2. **Situation Assessment and Messaging**

   - Convene an immediate fact-finding session. What happened, why, and who is affected? Draft initial holding statements within hours, even if details remain scarce.

3. **Stakeholder Mapping and Tiered Communication**

   - Identify primary audiences—customers, employees, investors, regulators, press—and craft tailored messages. Customers need troubleshooting guidance; employees need reassurance about job security; investors need impact assessments; regulators need compliance commitments.

4. **Communication Channels and Cadence**

   - Use multiple channels—email, website banners, social media, direct account outreach—to disseminate information. Commit to a regular update schedule until the crisis resolves, preventing message vacuum.

5. **Monitoring and Feedback Loop**

   - Track media coverage, social sentiment, customer support tickets, and employee morale. Adjust messaging and actions based on real-time feedback. Machiavelli valued intelligence networks; modern founders employ social listening tools and feedback dashboards.

6. **Post-Mortem and Narrative Reframing**

   - Once the immediate threat subsides, conduct a thorough post-mortem. Publicly share key learnings and policy changes. This reframes the crisis as an impetus for growth and reinforces your commitment to continuous improvement.

Example: Turning Crisis into Credibility

Imagine a fintech startup whose mobile app crashes during a major market downturn, leaving users unable to execute trades. A Machiavellian response would unfold thus:

- **Hour 1**: Issue a brief holding statement: "We are aware of outages affecting trading functionality and are working around the clock to resolve them."

- **Hour 3**: Provide status update: "Root cause identified: database overload. We are diverting traffic to our secondary data center and expect restoration within two hours."

- **Day 1**: Offer affected users fee credits, establish a dedicated support hotline, and publish a technical write-up explaining the fix.

- **Week 1**: Release a security and resilience roadmap, including third-party stress testing, redundancy upgrades, and a beta program for power users to validate upcoming releases.

- **Month 1**: Host a live Q&A with the CTO and CEO, transparently discussing lessons learned and product roadmaps. Invite user suggestions for resilience features.

- **Outcome**: Although the outage was damaging, the startup emerges with a reputation for accountability and technical rigor—qualities that attract institutional investors and large enterprise clients.

Conclusion of Chapter 5

Communication in entrepreneurship is command: the deliberate shaping of perception to align hearts, minds, and resources behind your vision. By crafting a founder story that resonates, deploying a disciplined PR and content strategy, balancing consistency with the agility your venture requires, and mastering crisis communication with transparency and speed, you seize control of your narrative battlefield. Machiavelli's enduring lesson is that power thrives where perception is managed with wisdom and resolve. In the next chapter, we will examine how leadership styles and organizational structures translate that narrative command into sustainable action on the ground.

Chapter 6: Leadership Styles and Structures

In *The Prince*, Machiavelli teaches that the art of rulership hinges not only on strategic cunning but on the skillful management of human loyalties. He writes that "a prince must learn how not to be good, and to use this knowledge or not according to necessity," emphasizing that effective leadership requires the deft balancing of fear, love, and respect. For entrepreneurs, these same dynamics play out daily: motivating teams, forging advisory relationships, structuring decision-making, and embedding cultural rituals. In this chapter, we explore how founders can wield these levers to galvanize high-performance organizations and build enduring institutions.

The Effectiveness of Fear, Love, and Respect in Teams

Machiavelli famously asserts that "it is better to be feared than loved, if you cannot be both." Yet he immediately qualifies that the optimal leader inspires both, for "men will sooner forget the death of their father than the loss of their patrimony." Translated to the startup context, this speaks to three distinct motivational currencies:

Fear as a Driver of Discipline

Fear—understood not as terror but as the binding certainty of consequences—can sharpen focus and ensure accountability. In Machiavelli's terms, a prince who fails to punish wrongdoing will see order give way to chaos: "Men are quick to change their allegiance when they see no penalty for disloyalty." Within a team, clear consequences for missing deadlines, violating budget guardrails, or breaching ethical standards reinforce standards of conduct. Fear of losing one's role or reputation, when applied judiciously, discourages slack and upholds excellence.

Yet fear alone can poison culture if overused. When team members feel perpetually threatened, creativity dries up and morale crumbles. Machiavelli warns that "a ruler who is feared yet unloved is sustained only by a dread of punishment, and when danger is past he is despised rather than missed." Entrepreneurs must therefore calibrate fear—using it to enforce non-negotiable commitments, but never so broadly that it stifles innovation.

Love as a Source of Alignment

Love—manifested as genuine care, empathy, and shared purpose—fuels discretionary effort and loyalty beyond contractual obligations. Machiavelli acknowledges that "men love at their own free will, but they fear at the command of the prince," suggesting that love, unlike fear, cannot be commanded but must be cultivated. Founders who invest in people—listening to concerns, supporting personal growth, celebrating milestones—ignite an emotional bond that sustains performance through inevitable hardships.

In practice, love-driven leadership shows up as mentoring conversations, flexible support for life's challenges, and transparent sharing of the company's journey—victories and setbacks alike. When employees feel seen and valued, they become ambassadors for the mission, often going the extra mile without prompt. However, love without boundaries risks collapsing standards: without the deterrent of consequences, a culture of comfort can erode urgency and discipline.

Respect as the Unifying Force

Between fear and love lies respect: the recognition of a leader's competence, integrity, and fairness. Machiavelli emphasizes that respect endures where love falters: "men respect him who inspires respect in them." Respect is earned through consistency—delivering on promises, applying standards impartially, and demonstrating expertise under pressure. A founder who steps into the trenches during crucial deadlines, who owns mistakes openly, and who rewards merit swiftly cultivates deep respect.

Respect creates durable alignment: team members trust that when times grow tough, their leader's decisions will be guided by principle, not whim. This offers the stability needed to navigate rapid growth or market upheaval. Unlike fear, respect does not require punitive reinforcement; unlike love, it does not demand constant emotional labor. It sits at the intersection of admiration and accountability, anchoring culture in shared confidence.

Balancing the Triad

The most effective leaders blend these three modalities dynamically. In the early days, tighter deadlines and higher stakes may call for firmer enforcement—leaning into the "fear" end of the spectrum to build discipline. As the organization matures, demonstrating empathy and personal investment fosters retention and creativity. Throughout, displaying competence and fairness underpins respect. Machiavelli's counsel—that "a prince must avoid being hated"—reminds founders to ensure that fear never descends into cruelty, that love never swerves into indulgence, and that respect never slips into aloofness.

Building Governing Councils: Advisory Boards and Mentors

Even the savviest prince surrounds himself with wise counselors. Machiavelli notes that a ruler who "chooses ignorant or corrupt advisers, chooses them to ruin him." For startups, the governing council often takes the form of an advisory board and a network of mentors. These bodies extend a founder's vision, shore up blind spots, and lend legitimacy to the venture.

The Role of an Advisory Board

An advisory board is a semi-formal group of seasoned professionals who convene at regular intervals to offer strategic guidance. Unlike a legally empowered board of directors, an advisory board wields influence but not votes. This structure offers several advantages:

1. **Diverse Expertise:** Invite individuals with complementary backgrounds—veteran operators, former regulators, domain specialists—so that each meeting unearths fresh

perspectives.

2. **Rapid Feedback:** In Machiavellian terms, these advisors serve as indispensable "eyes and ears," providing input on emerging threats and opportunities before they become crises.

3. **Network Access:** Advisors often open doors to partnerships, customers, or investors, much like a prince leveraging noble alliances to muster troops.

4. **Credibility Signal:** The mere presence of respected figures on your advisory board signals to stakeholders that your venture is taken seriously.

To structure an effective advisory board, define clear charters: meeting cadence, degree of confidentiality, compensation (equity, honoraria, or none), and expectations for active engagement. Like Machiavelli's ideal counselor—wise yet subservient to the prince's ultimate authority—advisors should challenge assumptions without overriding the founder's decision-rights.

The Power of Mentorship

Mentors differ from board members in their informality and immediacy. They are the elder statesmen or women whom founders consult one-on-one, often in unstructured settings. Machiavelli valued the sapientia of tutors and guardians in shaping a young prince's judgment; similarly, founders benefit from mentors who have weathered analogous journeys.

Effective mentorship relationships share key traits:

- **Psychological Safety:** Founders must feel free to surface vulnerabilities—cash-flow anxieties, product doubts, team conflicts—without fear of judgment.

- **Mutual Commitment:** Although mentees often initiate contact, mentors contribute not out of obligation but out of genuine investment in the founder's growth.

- **Reciprocity Over Time:** While mentors give wisdom, founders repay by delivering updates on progress, soliciting feedback, and sometimes assisting mentors in their own ventures or causes.

To cultivate these ties, founders should actively seek out mentors at industry gatherings, through incubator networks, or via warm introductions. They should also recognize when a mentor's advice falls outside their domain or when the relational fit shifts, gracefully pivoting to new guides as their venture evolves.

Delegation vs. Centralization—Finding the Optimal Balance

Machiavelli observes that a prince who attempts to oversee every detail will exhaust both himself and his resources: "He who is his own preceptor does not often come to good." Yet he warns that abdication of authority invites disorder. Entrepreneurs face a comparable tension: how much authority to centralize in the founder's hands, and how much to delegate to growing teams.

The Case for Centralization in Early Stages

In the seed and early growth phases, centralization offers coherence and speed. When the founder underwrites critical decisions—product direction, lead assembly hire, major pivot announcements—the venture moves with singular purpose. Machiavelli lauds "the prince who endures the weariness of governing in order that his followers may be safe and free," underscoring that hands-on leadership, while taxing, establishes a foundation of aligned intent.

The Imperative for Delegation as Scale Arrives

As headcount climbs and functions multiply, the founder's capacity for detail management reaches a limit. Attempting to micromanage product specs, sales negotiations, and marketing campaigns simultaneously leads to bottlenecks and burnout. Machiavelli counsels that "the prince ought to select wise men for his counsellors, and if the prince does not himself understand, at least his counsellors should." In startup terms, that means building leadership tiers—functional heads who translate the founder's vision into operational execution.

Delegation must be deliberate:

1. **Define Decision Rights:** Use a RACI matrix or decision-making framework to specify which roles own which choices. This creates clarity and prevents the "reply-all" paralysis that drags even simple matters through

endless review.

2. **Empower Through Context:** Rather than simply issuing directives, founders should share the full context—market data, customer feedback, financial constraints—so delegated leaders can make aligned judgments.

3. **Establish Guardrails:** Set non-negotiable boundaries—compliance standards, budget limits, core values—beyond which leaders must escalate. This maintains strategic coherence without smothering autonomy.

Dynamic Rebalancing

Neither pure centralization nor unfettered delegation is sustainable. Machiavelli's ideal prince constantly recalibrates, "seeking to husband both the activity of command and the spontaneity of counsel." Founders should similarly revisit their leadership structure at key inflection points—post-fundraise, pre–product launch, during major pivots—and adjust the balance of control accordingly.

Leadership Rituals and Symbols that Reinforce Culture

Beyond formal structures, Machiavelli recognized the subtle power of ritual and symbolism in binding subjects' loyalties. He writes of princes who "secured the affections of their people by their public works and benefactions," underscoring that what is seen and celebrated cements allegiance. For startups, intentional rituals and symbolic acts embed culture, clarify values, and maintain unity as the organization scales.

Rituals of Recognition and Belonging

- **All-Hands Ceremonies:** A weekly or biweekly gathering where teams share wins, surface challenges, and hear directly from leadership. These forums reinforce transparency and collective purpose. Machiavelli would liken them to court assemblies where the prince displayed his generosity and heard public petitions.

- **Milestone Celebrations:** Marking product launches, major customer wins, or funding rounds with shared experiences—hackathons, offsite retreats, or simple team lunches—imbues work with meaning beyond the daily grind.

- **Learning Sessions:** Instituting "failure postmortems" or "innovation showcases" elevates continuous improvement as a core value, signaling that experimentation—and its lessons—are celebrated.

Symbols of Identity

- **Physical Spaces:** Office design, from open-plan collaboration zones to quiet focus rooms, conveys cultural priorities (collaboration vs. concentration). Machiavelli understood that the architecture of a fortress sent signals of strength; startups, too, communicate values through space.

- **Artifacts and Apparel:** Custom swag—hoodies, stickers, badges—creates visible tokens of belonging. When employees wear company logos with pride at conferences or online, they become walking ambassadors of your culture.

- **Narrative Icons:** Founder anecdotes ("the midnight pizza pivot"), product mascots, or branded metaphors ("we are explorers charting unknown seas") embed shared stories into the collective psyche.

Sustaining Rituals Through Growth

As headcount swells, personal rituals risk becoming perfunctory. Machiavelli warns that "a ruler who forgets his beginnings is soon overwhelmed by hubris." Founders must therefore:

1. **Delegate Ritual Stewardship:** Appoint "culture champions" or "Ritual Masters" on each team to own the planning and evolution of rituals, ensuring they remain relevant and resonant.

2. **Solicit Collective Input:** Periodically survey teams on which traditions energize them and which feel stale, then adapt rituals to reflect the organization's evolving identity.

3. **Embed Rituals in Onboarding:** Introduce new hires early to key rituals—first all-hands, cultural kickoff events—so that culture is learned, not merely told.

Conclusion of Chapter 6

Leadership in entrepreneurship mirrors Machiavelli's dynamic vision of princely rule: a constant interplay of imposing discipline, inspiring devotion, and commanding respect. By understanding when to wield fear, nurture love, and earn respect; by assembling councils of advisors and mentors who broaden insight; by calibrating the tension between delegation and central control; and by weaving rituals and symbols into the fabric of daily life, founders build organizations that are both resilient and adaptive. These structures and practices transform leadership from a solo burden into a shared expedition—one in which every team member becomes invested in the venture's destiny, guided by the enduring wisdom of Machiavelli's *The Prince*.

Chapter 7: Competition and Conflict

In the theater of Renaissance Italy, princes jostled for territory, influence, and survival. Machiavelli observed that "war ought to be the study of a prince," for only those who understand conflict can hope to prevail in its crucible. In entrepreneurship, competition is the ever-present battlefield: rivals vie for customers, partners, talent, and capital. Conflict arises not only in the marketplace but also within legions of suppliers, regulators, and shifting alliances. Mastering competition demands disciplined analysis, strategic positioning, ethical judgment, and the savvy use of intelligence to anticipate and outmaneuver opponents.

In this chapter, we explore four pillars of competitive mastery:

1. **Identifying rivals and assessing their strengths**

2. **Offensive vs. defensive strategies in market competition**

3. **Ethical considerations: when to compete and when to flee**

4. **Leveraging competitive intelligence for strategic advantage**

By integrating Machiavelli's timeless insights with modern business realities, founders learn to treat competition not as a zero-sum scramble but as a measured contest in which foresight, adaptability, and principle yield lasting advantage.

1. Identifying Rivals and Assessing Their Strengths

Machiavelli warns princes that "a wise prince ought to observe all those things that make for his advantage, and abstain from the contrary," reminding leaders that deep knowledge of adversaries is foundational. Entrepreneurs must map the competitive landscape with similar rigor, distinguishing direct competitors from indirect substitutes, potential entrants, and even unlikely allies whose shifting priorities could render them adversaries overnight.

Mapping the Competitive Arena

Begin by sketching concentric circles of competition:

- **Core Rivals**: Companies offering nearly identical solutions to the same target customers. They occupy the closest ring and demand the most urgent analysis.

- **Adjacent Competitors**: Firms with overlapping features or customer segments—perhaps a project-management tool that edges into the collaboration space or a premium SaaS vendor eyeing SMB budgets.

- **Substitutes**: Alternative approaches to the same problem—spreadsheets for project tracking, freelance consultants for operational support, in-house teams rather than outsourcing.

- **Potential Entrants**: Large incumbents, nimble startups, or cross-industry players who might pivot into your domain if incentives align.

Machiavelli counsels that "the first method for estimating the intelligence of a ruler is to look at the men he has around him," illustrating the principle that situational awareness emerges as much from one's network as from desk research. In startup terms, this means supplementing public data—market reports, financial filings, press releases—with insights from customers, sales teams, and even former employees of rivals who know their inner workings.

Assessing Strengths and Vulnerabilities

Once rivals are identified, analyze them across dimensions that shape competitive power:

1. **Resource Base**

   - Financial reserves and funding runway

   - Technology assets, patents, proprietary algorithms

   - Brand recognition and customer loyalty

2. **Operational Capabilities**

   - Speed of product development and release cadence

- Distribution networks and channel partnerships

    - Talent pools and organizational structure

3. **Strategic Positioning**

    - Pricing and cost structures

    - Value propositions: are they competing on cost, differentiation, or niche specialization?

    - Go-to-market tactics: direct sales, self-serve freemium, partner-led

4. **Cultural and Leadership Factors**

    - The agility of decision-making processes

    - Leadership's appetite for risk and innovation

    - Employee morale and turnover rates

Machiavelli would remind us that "men change princes not because of the goodness of the new, but because of the resentment toward the old." In business, customers defect not always because a competitor offers more features, but because they feel neglected or undervalued. Thus, part of assessing rivals is scrutinizing their customer satisfaction levels, channel support responsiveness, and historical missteps.

Tools and Techniques for Rival Analysis

- **Win/Loss Reviews**: After sales engagements, interview prospects who chose rivals to understand decision drivers and perceived gaps.

- **Mystery Shopping and Product Trials**: Sign up for competitor products to experience onboarding, feature sets, pricing transparency, and support quality firsthand.

- **Social Listening and Review Sites**: Aggregate feedback from forums, app stores, and professional networks where customers voice praise and complaints.

- **Financial and Patent Filings**: Publicly traded companies must disclose major investments; patents reveal R&D focus areas.

By combining quantitative data with qualitative nuance, founders build a nuanced picture of each rival's true strengths and the vulnerabilities that can be targeted.

---

2. Offensive vs. Defensive Strategies in Market Competition

Machiavelli teaches that "one ought to entrench himself behind fortifications that he himself has erected," illustrating the importance of defensive preparations even as a prince contemplates conquest. Entrepreneurs, too, must craft both offensive and defensive strategies—knowing when to seize initiative and when to guard gains against encroachment.

Offensive Strategies: Seizing the Initiative

Offensive competition is about expansion—gaining share, entering new segments, and unsettling incumbents before they can respond. Key offensive tactics include:

1. **First-Mover Exploits**

   - **Category Creation**: Define a new niche for which you can claim proprietary "first" status—"the first AI-powered underwriting platform for microloans," for example. This attracts attention and builds STF (sea-to-sea) mindshare.

   - **Rapid Geographic Rollout**: Launch in adjacent markets faster than rivals can mobilize local partnerships, locking in early adopters and establishing local network effects.

2. **Value-Overload Campaigns**

   - **Freemium and Free Trials**: Offer generous feature sets at no cost to seed viral usage, then monetize power users. Machiavelli would liken this to giving small benefits liberally and often so that gratitude grows.

   - **Aggressive Pricing**: Temporarily undercut incumbents to destabilize their cost structures, forcing them to choose between margin erosion or conceding share.

3. **Disruptive Innovation**

   - **Platform Shifts**: Develop a fundamentally different technical architecture—serverless, decentralized, or mobile-first—that solves persistent pain points for users.

   - **Ecosystem Orchestration**: Build open APIs that attract third-party developers, creating network effects that incumbents cannot replicate quickly.

4. **Guerrilla Marketing and Partnerships**

   - **Co-Marketing Blitzes**: Form alliances with non-competing but complementary startups—every joint webinar or eBook doubles exposure.

   - **Influencer and Community Engagement**: Leverage micro-influencers and niche community leaders to seed word-of-mouth in verticals where incumbents have weak presence.

Offense demands boldness and calculated risk. Machiavelli applauds princes who "strike while the iron is hot," reminding entrepreneurs to capitalize on momentum—whether a successful funding round, a favorable regulatory shift, or a competitor misstep—before conditions change.

Defensive Strategies: Fortifying Your Position

Just as a prince builds walls and garrisons to hold acquired territory, startups must erect defenses to preserve their gains and deter rival incursions. Defensive measures include:

1. **Deepening Customer Relationships**

    - **Loyalty Programs and Long-Term Contracts**: Incentivize continued usage through tiered benefits, service credits, and multi-year commitments.

    - **Community Cultivation**: Create user forums, VIP advisory councils, and exclusive events where customers feel invested in the product's evolution.

2. **Technical Moats**

    - **Data Network Effects**: As more customers use your platform, the aggregated data insights become increasingly valuable—raising the bar for rivals.

    - **Integration Ecosystems**: Tight integrations with partner platforms make it costly for customers to switch.

3. **Operational Barriers**

    - **Complexity Lock-In**: Gradually introduce advanced modules that require specialized training, making migration to another vendor disruptive.

- **Regulatory and Compliance Expertise**: Achieve certifications—ISO, SOC 2, HIPAA—that reassure enterprise buyers and create a barrier for less-funded challengers.

4. **Intellectual Property Shields**

   - **Patent Portfolios**: File patents on core innovations to dissuade copycats and establish licensing opportunities.

   - **Trade Secrets and Proprietary Processes**: Document and secure key algorithms, data-preparation techniques, and customer-onboarding scripts.

Machiavelli stressed that a prince who relies solely on fortresses is vulnerable if he neglects the morale and loyalty of his people. Likewise, startups cannot erect technical moats without simultaneously nurturing customer trust and a culture of continuous improvement.

Choosing the Right Balance

Offense and defense are not mutually exclusive; they form a dynamic continuum. Early-stage startups, racing to establish product-market fit, often lean heavily on offense—experimenting rapidly and seeking to outpace rivals. As they gain traction, defensive investments become crucial to preserve hard-won ground.

To decide when to switch gears:

- **Monitor Market Signals**: A sudden glut of copycat entrants or aggressive pricing wars may call for defensive fortification.

- **Assess Resource Runway**: Defense typically requires sustained investment (engineering, compliance, customer success), so ensure funding stability before doubling down.

- **Gauge Cultural Readiness**: Teams accustomed to rapid feature releases may chafe under the slower pace of defensive projects; align incentives accordingly.

Machiavelli would endorse a ruler whose "eye is always turned to the internal well-being of the state" even as he contemplates new conquests. Similarly, founders must balance external expansion with internal resilience.

---

3. Ethical Considerations: When to Compete and When to Flee

Machiavelli's reputation as a cynic overshadows his nuanced advice on ethics: he acknowledges that "the ends justify the means" only in the austere calculus of statecraft, not as a carte blanche for unrestrained cruelty. For entrepreneurs, competition must be waged within ethical bounds that preserve reputation, stakeholder trust, and long-term viability. Sometimes the wisest course is not to fight, but to withdraw.

Ethics in Offensive and Defensive Tactics

- **Truthful Representation**: Machiavelli warns that deceived subjects resent their ruler. Misleading marketing claims or hidden fees may win short-term gains but sow distrust and regulatory scrutiny.

- **Fair Play vs. Dirty Tricks**: While Machiavelli accepted covert action—bribery, espionage—he did so in the service of stability. In business, covertly poaching trade secrets, launching smear campaigns, or orchestrating patent litigation purely to burden rivals damages industry credibility and invites legal backlash.

Recognizing When to Retreat

There are moments when continued engagement is not valor but folly:

1. **Unwinnable Battles**: When a competitor controls unassailable assets—market share, distribution exclusivity, regulatory favor—a direct confrontation may bleed resources without altering the outcome.

2. **Misaligned Core Values**: If a market's ethical or cultural norms contradict your company's principles—excessive data exploitation, predatory pricing models—entering that arena risks compromising core identity.

3. **Resource Overextension**: Chasing every segment, geography, or feature may spread the team so thin that the

venture's competitive advantage erodes across the board.

Machiavelli counsels that "a prudent ruler will always find the safest retreat," preserving his state's integrity even if it means ceding small tracts. Entrepreneurs must feel no shame in backward-integrating away from non-core markets or sunsetting unprofitable lines—especially when resources can be redeployed to higher-return initiatives.

Ethical Exit and Communication

When withdrawing:

- **Communicate Transparently**: Explain the rationale to affected customers or partners, offering smooth transitions, data portability, or recommended alternatives.

- **Honor Obligations**: Fulfill contractual commitments or negotiate fair settlements—abrupt breach of trust generates lasting reputational harm.

- **Preserve Bridges**: Former markets and partners may still align with future products; leaving on professional terms keeps doors open.

By balancing competitive ambition with ethical restraint, founders build not only profitable businesses but industries grounded in trust and respect.

4. Leveraging Competitive Intelligence for Strategic Advantage

In Machiavelli's era, reliable spies and informants furnished princes with the early warning signs of rebellion, invasion, or faltering alliances. Today's entrepreneurs require their own intelligence networks to detect shifts in competitor strategy, emerging technologies, and changing customer sentiment. The key lies in gathering accurate data legally and ethically, then translating insights into decisive action.

Building an Intelligence System

1. **Human Intelligence (HUMINT)**

   - **Customer Conversations**: Sales and support teams routinely hear competitor mentions, feature requests, and pricing complaints—create mechanisms to capture and analyze these qualitative signals.

   - **Industry Forums and Conferences**: Attend panels where competitors speak; glean hints of roadmap priorities or partnerships.

   - **Channel Partner Feedback**: Resellers and integrators often juggle multiple vendor relationships and can provide comparative assessments.

2. **Open-Source Intelligence (OSINT)**

   - **Web Scraping and Monitoring**: Track competitor websites for product updates, job postings signaling new initiatives, and investor presentations revealing strategic pivots.

   - **Social Media and Developer Platforms**: Follow GitHub, Twitter, and LinkedIn for signals on open-source contributions, tech stack changes, or hiring blitzes.

   - **Regulatory Filings and Public Data**: FDA approvals, data-protection registers, or patent office publications often foreshadow product launches or compliance investments.

3. **Technical Intelligence (TECHINT)**

   - **Code Analysis**: With permission, integrate competitor SDKs or APIs in sandbox environments to reverse-engineer capabilities.

   - **Security and Performance Benchmarks**: Use load-testing tools to gauge service resilience; vulnerability scanning can reveal architectural weaknesses.

4. **Competitive Benchmarking**

   - **Feature Matrices and Performance Charts**: Systematically compare key metrics—response times, pricing tiers, user limits—across products.

- ○ **User Sentiment Analysis**: Quantify star ratings, net promoter scores, and thematic sentiment from reviews to detect emerging pain points and opportunities.

Machiavelli would applaud the prince who "keeps his ear close to the ground," yet cautions that raw intelligence yields no power unless acted upon swiftly and strategically.

Converting Intelligence into Action

- **Strategic Alerts**: Establish thresholds—competitor price cuts beyond X percent, a surge in job postings for a new R&D center—that trigger leadership review and rapid response protocols.

- **Scenario Planning**: For each major intelligence insight, develop contingency plans—counter-offer promotions, accelerate feature roadmaps, adjust marketing positioning.

- **Cross-Functional War Rooms**: Assemble product, marketing, sales, and finance in rapid-reaction teams to digest intelligence and coordinate unified responses. Machiavelli emphasized that "he who wishes to be obeyed must know how to command," and commanding in crises demands clear, centralized coordination without stifling frontline initiative.

Maintaining Ethical Boundaries

While Machiavelli tolerated espionage as a tool of statecraft, modern enterprises must respect legal and ethical constraints:

- **No Industrial Espionage**: Avoid illicit methods—hacking, bribery, or confidential document theft—that expose the company to legal risk and moral reproach.

- **Respect Privacy Laws**: When scraping data or monitoring social channels, comply with terms of service and data-protection regulations.

- **Transparent Partnerships**: If leveraging third-party intelligence vendors, ensure their practices align with your company's ethical standards.

By weaving intelligence into the strategic fabric—just as Machiavelli's ideal prince wove informants into every layer of government—entrepreneurs anticipate rival moves, pre-empt threats, and seize fleeting opportunities.

Conclusion of Chapter 7

In competition and conflict, Machiavelli's counsel remains starkly relevant: leaders must know their rivals as well as they know themselves, wield offense and defense with equal finesse, temper ambition with ethical judgment, and invest in intelligence networks that illuminate the paths of both danger and opportunity. For entrepreneurs, victory lies not in crushing every competitor, but in sustaining a continuous edge—through agility, foresight, and integrity—that secures market leadership and fuels enduring growth. In the next chapter, we turn from the struggle against rivals to the choreography of influence—how founders command resources, shape perceptions, and marshal the instruments of power to advance their domains.

Chapter 8: Power Plays in Funding

In *The Prince*, Machiavelli reminds us that "a prince never lacks legitimate reasons to break his promise" when necessity demands it, yet he must wield such power judiciously to maintain his realm. For entrepreneurs, raising and managing capital is a series of power plays: securing the resources to build an enterprise, negotiating terms that preserve control and future upside, stewarding investors' confidence, and leveraging scarcity and urgency to sharpen deal terms. In this chapter, we delve into four essential aspects of funding strategy: choosing among equity, debt, and alternative financing; negotiating valuation, control, and exit rights; managing investor relations with transparency and discipline; and deploying scarcity and urgency to capture superior terms.

Raising Capital: Equity, Debt, and Alternative Financing

Before a prince wields armies, he must secure the treasury. Machiavelli counsels that "the true foundation of all states…is good laws and good arms," and in a startup context, "good arms" require the capital to hire talent, build product, and market effectively. Entrepreneurs face a spectrum of financing sources, each with distinct trade-offs in cost, control, and flexibility.

Equity Financing

Equity capital—selling ownership stakes in exchange for cash—remains the lifeblood of high-growth ventures. By issuing shares to angel investors, venture capitalists, or strategic partners, founders acquire runway to scale rapidly without incurring interest charges or mandatory repayments. Yet equity dilutes ownership, potentially eroding the founder's decision-making power over successive rounds.

- **Early Angels and Seed Rounds:** In the initial phases, founders often tap friends, family, and angel networks. Here, valuations are driven more by narrative and promise than by hard metrics. Machiavelli observed that "men in general judge more from appearances than from reality," underscoring the need to craft a compelling vision that persuades early backers to trade cash for potential.

- **Venture Capital:** As traction emerges, institutional investors perform rigorous due diligence, scrutinizing unit economics, founder backgrounds, and market potential. In exchange for deep pockets and operational support, they demand significant governance rights—board seats, protective provisions, and liquidation preferences.

- **Strategic Equity Partners:** Corporations may invest for strategic alignment—access to new technology or entry into adjacent markets. Such partners bring distribution channels and domain expertise, but also the risk of conflicting agendas if their corporate priorities shift.

Equity rounds must be timed to milestones—product-market fit, regulatory clearances, or major customer wins. A Machiavellian founder respects that "fortune favors the bold" but also knows when a safer path preserves too much control to pass up.

Debt Financing

Debt capital—loans, lines of credit, or convertible notes—allows founders to raise funds without immediate dilution. Interest payments and repayment schedules impose discipline but create fixed obligations that can strain cash flow if growth stalls.

- **Bank Loans and Venture Debt:** Banks offer term loans against collateral, often requiring personal guarantees or property liens. Venture debt providers extend non-dilutive capital to startups with proven revenue, charging higher interest and warrants in lieu of equity.

- **Convertible Instruments:** Convertible notes or SAFEs defer valuation negotiations to a future round, accruing interest or discount to equity. Machiavelli's advice to "put safety before generosity" resonates: convertible vehicles provide quick cash while preserving flexibility on price discovery.

- **Revenue-Based Financing:** Lenders advance capital in exchange for a percentage of future revenues until a fixed multiple is repaid. This aligns repayment with performance but may prove costly if top-line grows faster than planned.

Debt suits businesses with stable cash flows and predictable working-capital needs. The prudent founder ensures that debt service never jeopardizes the ability to invest in strategic opportunities—a lesson Machiavelli would applaud: "He who is overly generous rests on uncertain foundations."

Alternative Financing

Beyond equity and debt, a growing array of options can fund innovation:

- **Grants and Subsidies:** Government programs, research institutions, and philanthropic foundations offer non-dilutive grants for technology development, social impact, or underserved markets. Such funds require rigorous reporting but confer credibility and cushion cash burn.

- **Crowdfunding:** Platforms like Kickstarter or Indiegogo allow pre-selling products to gauge demand and secure capital without giving up equity. Rewards-based crowdfunding builds early communities but demands fulfillment capabilities and can cap price flexibility.

- **Revenue Pre-Sales and Customer Financing:** Large enterprise customers may fund product development in exchange for favorable pricing or exclusivity. Machiavelli recognized that "it is necessary to know how to disguise one's intentions," warning that founders must manage such deals carefully to avoid dependency or misaligned expectations.

- **Tokenization and ICOs:** Blockchain ventures raise funds by issuing digital tokens, blending utility with speculative appeal. These models can generate vast sums quickly but confront regulatory uncertainty and token-value volatility.

The ideal financing mix depends on the venture's capital intensity, time horizon, and appetite for dilution. A Machiavellian approach balances the desire for growth with the imperative to preserve strategic flexibility and founder agency.

Terms Negotiation: Valuation, Control, and Exit Rights

Securing capital is only half the battle; the terms you agree to shape the venture's trajectory. Machiavelli teaches that "he who becomes prince by the favor of the people ought to keep them friendly," highlighting that early supporters' alignment is as crucial as their financial backing. Founders must negotiate valuation, control provisions, and exit rights with care, ensuring that incentives align and authority remains sufficiently concentrated.

Valuation

Valuation sets the price of equity and determines dilution: a higher pre-money valuation means less equity the company must part with. Founders must balance ambition with realism:

- **Traction-Based Benchmarks:** Anchor negotiations in tangible metrics—monthly recurring revenue, customer growth rates, gross margin trends—to justify valuation multiples aligned with public comparables or recent sector financing.

- **Narrative Premium:** Machiavelli would appreciate using narrative to shape perception: if you can convincingly articulate a multibillion-dollar market opportunity and your unique positioning within it, investors may assign a premium, despite early revenue.

- **Down Rounds and Flat Rounds:** When growth lags expectations, a down round can inject cash but devastate morale and valuation benchmarks. Flat rounds preserve value but may signal to the market that progress has stalled. Founders must weigh the cost of dilution against the cost of scarring their cap table.

Ultimately, valuation negotiations hinge on power dynamics: the more competitive investor interest you can solicit, the stronger your hand—echoing Machiavelli's insight that "men are more apt to be influenced by the assurance of the majority than by the voice of a few."

Control Provisions

Investors seek safeguards to protect their capital and influence strategic decisions. Founders should aim to retain founder-friendly governance while granting investors comfort that their interests are represented.

- **Board Composition:** Negotiate the ratio of founder, investor, and independent directors. A board dominated by investors may steer strategy away from the founder's vision; too few independent seats can leave critical disputes unresolved.

- **Protective Rights and Vetoes:** Investors often demand veto rights over future financings, budget approvals, or major corporate actions. Machiavelli recognized that a prince must "prevent conspiracy…by controlling the commanders and captains," analogous to careful allocation of veto power to avoid insurrection but ensure prudent oversight.

- **Founder Vesting and Cliffs:** To align incentives, founders typically vest their remaining shares over time or upon achievement of milestones. This protects investors if a founder departs prematurely but can be structured to reward early achievements.

- **Drag-Along and Tag-Along Rights:** Drag-along provisions ensure minority shareholders must sell in a qualified exit; tag-along rights protect minorities by allowing them to join a sale on equal terms. These clauses balance exit efficiency with minority protections.

Skilled negotiators frame each control provision as mutual protection: investors guard their downside; founders guard the venture's mission against well-intentioned but potentially misaligned oversight.

Exit Rights

Investors want a clear path to liquidity; founders want to preserve optionality. Common exit-related terms include:

- **Liquidation Preferences:** Determine the order and multiple at which investors recoup proceeds before common shareholders participate. A 1× preference returns invested capital; a 2× preference doubles it. "Participating" preferences add further complexity. Founders must ensure preferences do not unduly compress founders' eventual upside.

- **Redemption Rights:** Some investors negotiate the right to demand redemption of their shares after a defined period, forcing the company to buy back shares. While rare in early rounds, such clauses can become burdensome if growth stalls.

- **IPO Registration Rights:** Institutional investors may require management to register shares for a public offering when certain thresholds are met, which can compel an exit timeline that the founder may not favor.

- **ROFR and Co-Sale Rights:** Rights of first refusal and co-sale provisions allow investors to maintain proportional ownership in future liquidity events, preserving cap table structure but limiting founder flexibility in bringing on new strategic investors.

Machiavelli would warn that "a prince should never allow his soldiers to be deceived," reminding founders that the fine print of exit rights can shape incentives—and conflicts—for years to come.

Managing Investor Relations: Expectations and Accountability

Raising capital seals a covenant between founder and investor. Machiavelli affirms that "a prince ought to inspire his followers with such confidence that they will follow him to the death," a level of trust that startups must cultivate with their backers. Transparent communication, disciplined reporting, and pragmatic expectation-setting preserve goodwill even when the road roughens.

Establishing Communication Cadence

- **Regular Board Meetings:** Hold quarterly meetings with a clear agenda—review of financials, KPI updates, strategic roadmaps, and risk assessments. In Machiavellian fashion, these sessions serve both to inform and to reinforce the founder's command.

- **Monthly or Bi-Monthly Updates:** Distribute concise written reports detailing progress against plan, budget variances, hiring statistics, and competitive intelligence. Over-communication beats radio silence when performance lags.

- **Ad Hoc Alerts:** For material developments—major customer wins, regulatory issues, or leadership changes—send immediate alerts accompanied by clear action plans and support requests.

Aligning on Milestones and Metrics

Investors often tie future funding tranches to milestone achievements. Founders should negotiate realistic targets that reflect competitive and operational realities:

- **Milestone Clarity:** Frame metrics—revenue, user growth, churn rate, product roadmap completion—with specific definitions and data sources to avoid disputes over whether thresholds have been met.

- **Buffer Zones:** Build in headroom—set targets that you can surpass comfortably to create "win windows" for both sides. Machiavelli admired princes who "make victory in doubt always certain," a principle that applies to setting stretch but achievable goals.

- **Reforecast Mechanisms:** Agree on processes for updating plans when external factors shift—market downturns, supply-chain disruptions—so that capital deployment remains nimble and expectations stay grounded.

Building Credibility Through Transparency

When founders share both triumphs and trials candidly, investors gain confidence in the leadership team's judgment:

- **Pre-Mortems and Post-Mortems:** Before embarking on major initiatives, outline potential failure modes and mitigation plans. After setbacks, lead frank analyses of root causes and corrective actions. Machiavelli's ideal prince studies "the disposition of the troops and the condition of affairs," anticipating problems before they become crises.

- **Governance Discipline:** Uphold agreed financial controls—audited statements, expense policies, and compliance frameworks—demonstrating respect for investors' risk.

- **Constructive Engagement:** Solicit investor input on strategic choices where their domain expertise adds value, reinforcing their partnership role while retaining clear decision rights.

Over time, this governance rigor cements trust, reducing friction when hard decisions arise or when additional capital is needed.

Using Scarcity and Urgency to Secure Better Terms

Machiavelli understood that the prospect of rare opportunity compels action: "Nothing is more difficult to take in hand, nor more perilous to conduct," yet the allure of unique chance drives men to extraordinary lengths. Entrepreneurs can harness the dynamics of scarcity and urgency to tilt funding negotiations in their favor.

Cultivating Competitive Tension

- **Multiple Investor Processes:** Running simultaneous conversations with two or more investors creates leverage. The fear of missing out drives investors to accelerate diligence and sweeten terms.

- **Visible Traction Milestones:** Timed releases of impressive metrics—record user sign-ups, landmark partnerships—signal momentum that investors do not want to miss.

- **The "Closed Door" Strategy:** Indicate that you are nearing a decision, yet leave time for last-minute improvements. Machiavelli would applaud the art of "letting others know the prize while concealing one's exact hand."

Structuring Timelines

- **Short Windows for Term Sheets:** Give investors a defined period—five to ten business days—to deliver term sheets. This avoids drawn-out negotiations that erode leverage and urgency.

- **Milestone-Linked Increases:** Offer more attractive terms to investors who commit by an earlier cutoff, then adjust valuations or board seats after the window closes.

- **Preemptive Announcements:** Publicly announce that you plan to close a round by a specific date, prompting stakeholders to align their internal approval processes accordingly.

Signaling and Sealing the Deal

- **Soft Circle Notifications:** Inform later-stage investors that a lead has "committed in principle," which encourages them to move quickly.

- **Use of Data Rooms:** A well-organized data room with clean documentation and responsive Q&A signals preparedness and instills confidence that the deal will close smoothly.

- **Finality in Closing:** Once the round is sealed, Machiavelli's advice applies: "When a prince has conquered a republic and free city, he should destroy, ruin, and … transform it into a monarchy." In funding terms, you firm up board charters, vesting plans, and investor agreements immediately, leaving no ambiguity about the new governance structure.

By wielding scarcity and urgency artfully, founders can capture higher valuations, preserve control, and accelerate execution of their vision.

Conclusion of Chapter 8

Funding is the lifeblood of entrepreneurial conquest, but it is also a minefield of trade-offs. Machiavelli's razor-sharp insights remind founders that power—whether in politics or in startups—derives not from resources alone but from how those resources are secured, deployed, and managed. By understanding the nuances of equity, debt, and alternative financing; by negotiating valuation, control, and exit terms with strategic foresight; by nurturing investor relations with transparency and discipline; and by harnessing scarcity and urgency to sharpen deal terms, entrepreneurs command the capital they need without sacrificing the autonomy to wield it effectively. In the chapters ahead, we will explore the instruments of influence beyond funding—intelligence networks, alliances, and institutional structures—that transform a well-capitalized venture into an enduring principality in the marketplace.

Chapter 9: Intelligence and Information

In the unforgiving theater of Renaissance power struggles, Machiavelli teaches that knowledge is as vital to a prince as armies and fortifications. "A prudent ruler never occupies himself entirely with either affairs: he devotes part of his attention to them both," he writes, underscoring the importance of both action and awareness. For entrepreneurs, the art of intelligence and information is no less critical: building networks that feed real-time insight into every corner of the venture; harnessing customer and market data to guide decisions; defending vital secrets against industrial espionage; and stewarding data ethically and in compliance with evolving regulations. In this chapter, we unpack four pillars of modern entrepreneurial intelligence:

1. **Building Your Information Networks and Feedback Loops**

2. **Customer Insights, Market Research, and Data-Driven Decisions**

3. **Counterintelligence: Protecting Trade Secrets and IP**

4. **Ethical Data Use and Compliance**

Through disciplined systems and Machiavellian foresight, founders transform raw signals into strategic advantage and ensure that the lifeblood of their organizations—information—flows unimpeded, accurate, and protected.

---

1. Building Your Information Networks and Feedback Loops

Machiavelli counsels that a prince must "see clearly and know thoroughly the condition of his troops and of the affairs of the state." In startups, where conditions can shift overnight, founders must erect robust information networks—internal and external—that surface opportunities and threats early, enabling rapid, informed responses. These networks rest on two pillars: channels that gather raw data, and feedback loops that turn data into decisions.

Internal Intelligence: From Frontline to Founder

Your organization itself is the richest source of intelligence. Sales teams, customer-success managers, engineers, and finance professionals all observe friction points, usage patterns, and emerging risks. But without structured channels, these observations dissipate as noise rather than coalesce into insight.

- **Regular "Truth-to-Power" Forums:** Machiavelli admired rulers who listened candidly to tough truths. Instituting monthly "all-hands retrospectives" where cross-functional teams surface blockers, battlefield lessons, and market rumors invites unvarnished feedback. Leaders must signal that airing bad news invites appreciation, not punishment, fostering psychological safety.

- **"Intelligence Champions" in Every Department:**
  Appoint a liaison in sales, product, operations, and support
  whose explicit role is to capture field
  intelligence—customer objections, emerging competitor
  moves, regulatory snatches—and feed it into a central "war
  room." These champions gather anecdotes, numeric
  reports, and first-party feedback in standardized templates.

- **Digital War Room Dashboards:** Modern startups employ
  real-time dashboards that ingest metrics—from user
  activity logs to support ticket trends—and present alert
  thresholds. When product errors spike, or churn edges up,
  the dashboard rings alarms. Machiavelli would nod at such
  corner towers of vigilance, ensuring the prince knows the
  pulse of every garrison.

- **Decision Cadence Meetings:** Intelligence without
  decision is wasted. Weekly leadership huddles review key
  metrics, debate recommended pivots, and commit to
  actions. Like a prince weighing the counsel of generals and
  ministers, founders must balance diverse inputs, then
  execute decisively.

External Intelligence: Allies, Rivals, and the Market

No principality exists in isolation. Entrepreneurs must listen
beyond their walls: to partners, customers, regulators, and even
competitors. External intelligence comprises both open channels
and discreet inquiries.

- **Customer Advisory Councils:** Invite trusted customers to periodic advisory sessions. Feedback on roadmaps, beta features, and support practices yields insights no survey can capture. Machiavelli praised rulers who consulted public assemblies selectively—here, the modern equivalent is a curated circle that shapes strategy.

- **Partner Ecosystem Forums:** If you integrate with major platforms or rely on channel partners, schedule quarterly partnership reviews. Beyond performance metrics, ask partners what upstream shifts they foresee—new compliance regimes, shifting end-customer demands, or technical roadblocks—that could ripple into your domain.

- **Competitive Listening Posts:** Monitor competitors' job postings, public filings, and developer activity. A surge in postings for "machine-learning engineers" signals a new technical push; a patent application hints at forthcoming features. These public breadcrumbs, when tracked diligently, provide early warning of rival strategies.

- **Regulatory and Policy Radar:** In highly regulated sectors—healthcare, finance, energy—regulator advisories, public comment dockets, and draft legislation represent crucial intelligence. Assign a regulatory affairs role to scan government websites and industry trade associations, summarizing changes that could enable or disable your business model.

Embedding Continuous Feedback

A hallmark of Machiavellian strategy is vigilance without paralysis. Feedback loops must be both continuous and lightweight, ensuring the organization senses shifts even as it pursues goals.

- **"Minimum Viable Metrics" Approach:** Rather than tracking dozens of vanity metrics, define a handful of leading indicators—customer activation rates, support escalations, net promoter scores—that correlate strongly with long-term success. Monitor these daily or weekly to spot inflection points.

- **Rapid A/B and Multivariate Testing:** Embed testing frameworks into your product and marketing, turning every user interaction into an experiment. Each campaign becomes a mini-battle, yielding data on what resonates—a modern reflection of Machiavelli's advice to "vary innovations gradually, so people grow accustomed to them."

- **Automated Alerts and Escalations:** Use rule-based triggers that push urgent anomalies—downtime, security alerts, social-media surges—to Slack channels or pager systems. This ensures the right teams respond before small sparks become conflagrations.

Building these networks and loops transforms raw events—customer complaints, rumor of a new competitor, regulatory whisper—into systematic inputs that guide resource allocation, product pivots, and communication strategies.

2. Customer Insights, Market Research, and Data-Driven Decisions

"A prince ought to have no other aim or thought, nor select anything else for his study, than war and its rules and discipline," Machiavelli instructs, emphasizing the primacy of deep domain expertise. For entrepreneurs, the equivalent discipline is mastering customer behaviors, market dynamics, and analytic techniques. Data alone does not guarantee wisdom; it must be contextualized, interrogated, and woven into narratives that spur action.

Customer Insights: Listening and Learning

Customers are the ultimate arbiters of value. Their feedback—explicit and implicit—must inform every strategic choice.

- **Voice-of-Customer Programs:** Structured processes for capturing NPS surveys, in-app feedback, and post-support interviews produce both quantitative scores and qualitative anecdotes. Machiavelli would recognize these as the prince's town criers—reporting citizens' pulse on the state of affairs.

- **Ethnographic Studies and User Shadowing:** Observing customers in their natural environments—offices, homes, retail floors—uncovers latent needs that clickstream data cannot reveal. Founders who shadow power users gain firsthand appreciation for workarounds, pain points, and heuristics that shape product design.

- **Churn and Renewal Analysis:** When customers leave, understanding why is as vital as celebrating successes. Segment churn by cohort, feature usage, and contract structure to detect patterns—perhaps support responsiveness, pricing inflexibility, or competitor lock-in are driving departures.

- **Customer Journey Mapping:** Chart the end-to-end experience—from initial awareness through purchase, onboarding, daily use, and renewal. Identify friction points where customers stall or falter. Like Machiavelli's generals charting siege approaches, entrepreneurs use journey maps to plan interventions that clear obstacles.

Market Research: Scanning the Broader Field

Internal signals must be calibrated against external realities. Market research disciplines guide the prince's understanding of geography; for startups, they illuminate market size, growth potential, and competitive contours.

- **Top-Down and Bottom-Up Sizing:** Combine macroeconomic data—industry reports, government statistics—with primary research—customer willingness-to-pay studies, pilot program conversions—to triangulate a realistic total addressable market. Machiavelli warns princes against overestimating one's resources; similarly, inflated TAMs lead to strategic overreach.

- **Trend Analysis and Scenario Forecasting:** Identify shifts in technology, regulation, and customer behavior that could reshape demand. Workshops that map alternative futures—best case, worst case, normative—prepare founders to adapt. As Machiavelli noted, "fortune is the ruler of one-half of our actions," but foresight mitigates the caprices of chance.

- **Competitive Landscape Profiling:** Build dynamic profiles of rivals' market shares, pricing tiers, distribution channels, and technology stacks. Use periodic mystery shopping and secondary research to update these profiles, enabling side-by-side comparisons that expose white-space opportunities.

- **Voice-of-Market Panels:** Engage panels of industry experts—analysts, consultants, seasoned customers—to validate assumptions, stress-test roadmaps, and anticipate regulatory headwinds. This reflects the Machiavellian practice of consulting wise counselors while retaining the prince's ultimate decision rights.

Data-Driven Decision Frameworks

Data fuels decisions, but only with discipline. Machiavelli would champion the prince who "pursues his ends with such efficiency that the success seems effortless," a state achieved when analytics guide action.

- **Hypothesis-Driven Experimentation:** Frame strategic questions as hypotheses—"if we lower onboarding steps by two screens, activation will rise 15%"—then design experiments to test them. Reject or refine strategies based on statistical significance rather than gut feel alone.

- **Decision Trees and Playbooks:** Document decision logic for recurring choices—pricing adjustments, feature prioritization, market entry—to accelerate responses and ensure consistency. Machiavelli knew that armies march best when drilled; startups execute fastest when protocols exist.

- **Data-Empowered OKRs:** Align Objectives and Key Results around measurable outcomes—monthly recurring revenue, trials converted, customer satisfaction improvements—and tie them to data sources. Leaders review OKRs weekly, using dashboards to track progress and pivot resource allocation as needed.

- **Risk and Confidence Intervals:** Every data point carries uncertainty. Quantify confidence levels—sample sizes, error margins—and incorporate them into decision criteria. Machiavelli admired the cautious prince who "acts with deliberation," avoiding rash moves on flimsy evidence.

By blending customer insight, rigorous research, and disciplined analytics, entrepreneurs steer with clarity, turning data into the compass that guides product roadmaps, go-to-market strategies, and operational investments.

3. Counterintelligence: Protecting Trade Secrets and IP

In Machiavelli's account, the prince's dominion crumbles when internal betrayal or enemy sabotage exposes vulnerabilities. "The first method for estimating the intelligence of a ruler is to look at the men he has around him," he writes, alluding to the risk posed by disloyal advisers. For startups, the parallel threat is industrial espionage: digitized supply chains, mobile workforces, and borderless talent markets create myriad channels through which critical secrets—algorithms, customer lists, manufacturing processes—can leak. Counterintelligence is the Silent Branch guard that secures intellectual property and proprietary know-how.

Identifying Key Assets and Vulnerabilities

Begin by cataloging what must be protected:

- **Core Algorithms and Source Code:** Machine-learning models, encryption routines, or proprietary protocols that underpin your value proposition.

- **Product Roadmaps and Design Specifications:** Early-stage concepts are particularly sensitive until legal protections are in place.

- **Customer and Partner Data:** Contact lists, contractual terms, bespoke integrations—data breaches here damage both reputation and competitive position.

- **Manufacturing and Supply-Chain Processes:**
  Specialized methods or materials that form cost or quality
  advantages.

Conduct a **threat model exercise** to map possible leak vectors:

- **Insider Risks:** Disgruntled employees, contractors, or
  departed executives who maintain knowledge and
  potentially access.

- **Third-Party Exposure:** Shared code repositories,
  outsourced development, cloud service configurations.

- **External Intercepts:** Phishing, malware, or physical
  breaches at offices or data centers.

Technical and Organizational Safeguards

- **Access Controls and Least Privilege:** Enforce
  role-based access, granting employees and contractors
  only the minimum permissions needed. Machiavelli prized
  strict boundaries between war councils and general
  audiences; startups likewise must segment sensitive
  information.

- **Secure Development Lifecycle (SDL):** Integrate security
  reviews, code signing, and penetration testing into every
  sprint. Automate static and dynamic analysis to catch
  vulnerabilities before code reaches production.

- **Non-Disclosure Agreements and IP Clauses:** While Machiavelli recognized that "promises made through force must be kept," modern counterparts rely on carefully drafted NDAs and IP-assignment clauses with employees and partners to create legal deterrents.

- **Data Encryption and Monitoring:** Encrypt data at rest and in transit. Monitor privileged account activities for anomalous downloads or exports, triggering alerts when unusual patterns emerge.

- **Offboarding Protocols:** When employees or contractors depart, immediately revoke all system access, recover hardware, and remind them of ongoing confidentiality obligations. Machiavelli would note the importance of swift, decisive action to prevent rumor mills from exploiting gaps.

- **Security Awareness Training:** Regularly educate teams on phishing, social engineering, and secure coding. A vigilant workforce serves as the first line of defense, akin to loyal sentries at a fortress gate.

Incident Response and Resilience

No fortress is impregnable. A pragmatic counterintelligence stance accepts that breaches may occur and prepares accordingly.

- **Incident Response Playbooks:** Predefine roles, communication plans, forensic procedures, and legal escalation paths. Machiavelli urged that "injury should be done all at once," meaning that containment must be swift to prevent prolonged damage.

- **Regular Penetration Tests and Red-Team Exercises:** Simulate adversarial attacks—both technical breaches and social-engineering ploys—to uncover cracks before real foes exploit them.

- **Insurance and Liability Planning:** Cyber-liability and IP-theft insurance provide financial remediation in case of successful intrusions, enabling recovery without bankruptcy.

By treating counterintelligence as a strategic priority—woven into culture, processes, and technology—founders safeguard the secrets that power competitive advantage and guard against subtle betrayals that could topple the state.

---

4. Ethical Data Use and Compliance

Machiavelli's realism can obscure his awareness of the limits beyond which tyranny breeds revolt. "He who becomes prince through the favor of the people ought to keep them friendly by not devoting himself to any of their harms." Today's entrepreneurs operate under a social contract: customers trust startups with their personal information and expect it to be used responsibly. Violations—whether through data breaches, privacy abuses, or discriminatory algorithms—invite regulatory punishment and public backlash, undermining the very legitimacy the venture strives to build.

Navigating the Regulatory Landscape

- **Global Privacy Regimes:** GDPR in Europe, CCPA in California, LGPD in Brazil, PDPA in Singapore—each law prescribes data-subject rights, breach notification timelines, and hefty fines. Machiavelli would remind a prince that laws serve both as shield and sword: compliance prevents sanction, and reputation as a "prince who honors his word" attracts more goodwill.

- **Sector-Specific Regulations:** Healthcare (HIPAA), finance (PCI DSS, GLBA), children's data (COPPA) impose stricter controls. Map applicable regimes early and assign accountability to a privacy officer or compliance lead.

- **Cross-Border Data Transfers:** Standard contractual clauses, binding corporate rules, and adequacy decisions govern transfers. Ignorance here can derail international expansions.

Embedding Ethical Principles

Legal compliance is a floor, not a ceiling. Leading startups adopt ethical frameworks to guide data use beyond mere legality.

- **Privacy by Design:** Integrate privacy considerations into product architecture—data minimization, pseudonymization, and user-consent mechanisms become default, not afterthoughts.

- **Algorithmic Fairness and Transparency:** For AI-driven offerings, establish processes to detect and mitigate bias. Provide customers with explanations of automated decisions and avenues for human review.

- **Responsible Data Sharing:** When monetizing data through partnerships, ensure anonymization and aggregation standards that prevent re-identification. Machiavelli's ideal prince might dispense patronage, but not at the expense of trust.

- **Ethics Boards and Review Panels:** Convene multidisciplinary councils—legal, technical, customer-advocacy—to vet novel data uses and anticipate societal impacts before launch.

Building Trust Through Openness

- **Transparent Privacy Policies:** Use plain-language explanations, interactive consent dashboards, and real-time notifications of policy changes. Machiavelli recognized that "a prince should appear to be merciful, faithful… and religious," implying that visible virtues foster loyalty.

- **Breach Notification Protocols:** When breaches occur, communicate swiftly—within 72 hours where mandated—detailing scope, remediation steps, and support resources. Delayed disclosures, even if technically legal, fracture trust irreparably.

- **Certifications and Attestations:** SOC 2, ISO 27001, or privacy-seal programs signal commitment to rigorous standards. These externally validated badges reassure customers and partners that data is guarded as a prince guards his realm.

Conclusion of Chapter 9

Information is the sinew that connects every part of the entrepreneurial enterprise. Machiavelli's teachings on vigilance, counsel, and calculated action echo across the centuries: a prince who neglects intelligence invites downfall; one who masters it secures lasting dominion. By building robust internal and external networks, converting raw customer and market data into disciplined decision frameworks, defending secrets with vigilant counterintelligence, and stewarding data ethically within compliance regimes, founders command the flows of knowledge that shape strategy, shield against threats, and reinforce legitimacy. Armed with these insights, entrepreneurs stand poised to navigate the fiercest competitive storms and chart their principalities toward enduring success.

Chapter 10: Institutionalizing Success

Building a successful startup is akin to conquering a principality; sustaining that success is the art of building enduring institutions. Machiavelli observes that a ruler who depends solely on his personal prowess risks collapse when he is gone: "Princes who have derived their states from the excellence of their own virtue and arms maintain them not by fortune, but by virtue." In entrepreneurial terms, the founder's charisma and hands-on leadership can ignite growth, but true longevity comes from embedding processes, structures, and leadership layers that outlast any individual. In this chapter, we explore four interconnected pillars of institutionalization:

1. From founder-centric to process-driven operations

2. Systems and Standard Operating Procedures (SOPs) that outlive key individuals

3. Cultivating second-line leaders and succession planning

4. Maintaining flexibility within structures

By translating Machiavellian principles into modern organizational practice, founders create principled, adaptive enterprises capable of scaling, weathering storms, and sustaining competitive advantage long after the founding team moves on.

From Founder-Centric to Process-Driven Operations

In a nascent principality, power radiates from a single center: the prince. Similarly, early-stage startups revolve around the founder's vision, energy, and decisions. Machiavelli recognizes that new princes must rely on their own abilities and arms: "He who becomes prince through his own arms and ability should keep his army made up of his own subjects." In a young company, those "subjects" are employees whose trust and loyalty hinge on personal relationships with the founder. But as the realm expands, centralization around a single figure becomes a liability: bottlenecks form, the founder is stretched thin, and the organization's vitality is endangered if that figure falters or departs.

Recognizing the Shift

The transition from founder-centric to process-driven typically unfolds in three stages:

1. **Ad hoc Beginnings**: In the first 10–20 people, processes are informal. Decisions happen over Slack or a quick meeting. Roles are fluid; employees wear multiple hats. Speed and experimentation matter more than consistency.

2. **Scaling Tension Point**: Beyond 50–100 people, conflicting priorities and duplicated efforts emerge. Onboarding becomes chaotic. Customer experiences vary wildly by account manager. The founder's inbox bulges

with operational requests, distracting from high-level strategy.

3. **Process-Driven Maturity**: The company codifies key workflows—product development sprints, go-to-market launches, customer support escalations—into repeatable playbooks. Teams own their domains, empowered by clear inputs, outputs, and handoffs. Senior leaders translate the founder's principles into structure, freeing the founder to focus on vision, culture, and external relations.

Embedding Process without Killing Agility

Machiavelli extols the virtues of strong institutions yet warns that a rigid fortress can be stormed if its gates cannot adapt: "It is necessary for a prince wishing to hold his own to know how to do wrong." In organizational terms, processes must balance consistency with discretion. Five guiding principles help navigate this tension:

1. **Principles-Based Frameworks**
   Rather than dictating every detail, articulate principles—customer first, data-driven decisions, rapid learning—that guide behavior. Teams can then interpret these principles within their contexts, maintaining alignment without slavish compliance.

2. **Modular SOPs**
   Define standard operating procedures as discrete modules—"Lead Qualification," "Feature Prioritization," "Incident Response"—that teams can adopt or adapt.

Modules should specify objectives, core steps, decision criteria, and escalation paths. When contexts change, modules can be revised without redoing the entire process architecture.

3. **Embedded Feedback Mechanisms**
   Machiavelli applauds rulers who solicit intelligence before making major shifts. Embed feedback loops at every process boundary: retrospectives after go-lives, surveys after support cases, check-ins after onboarding. Use these inputs to refine workflows continuously.

4. **Process Owners and Champions**
   Assign accountability for each process to a named owner who monitors adherence, collects improvement suggestions, and updates documentation. These champions serve as guardians of process integrity and advocates for necessary evolution.

5. **Process Health Metrics**
   Track leading indicators—cycle time, handoff delays, error rates—and establish thresholds that trigger process health reviews. Machiavelli recognized that "fortune is the ruler of half our actions," but discipline reduces the role of chance. By monitoring process health, organizations can detect emerging dysfunctions before they catalyze crises.

By shifting from founder-centric reliance to process-driven rigor, startups preserve the benefits of entrepreneurial dynamism while laying foundations for scale and resilience.

Systems and SOPs That Outlive Key Individuals

Machiavelli stresses that "it is much safer to be feared than loved… for love is held by a chain of obligation which, men being selfish, is broken whenever it serves their purpose; but fear is maintained by a dread of punishment which never fails." Transposed to organizational design, this translates into the need for systems—rules, workflows, and technologies—that maintain consistent performance regardless of personnel changes. SOPs institutionalize best practices, ensuring that even when heroes leave, the machine continues to hum.

Building Durable Systems

1. **Document Everything**
   In the rush of execution, documentation is often deprioritized. Yet unrecorded processes live only in heads, vulnerable to attrition. Create living documents—wikis, playbooks, runbooks—that detail every critical workflow. Include context: purpose, inputs, outputs, responsible roles, and review cadences.

2. **Leverage Technology Platforms**
   Embed workflows in tools: ticketing systems for support, project management software for development, CRM for sales. Automate handoffs, notifications, and reports so that the system enforces process steps even if people rotate

roles.

3. **Standardize Onboarding and Training**
   New hires must learn both culture and process. Develop structured onboarding programs—self-paced e-learning, shadowing sprints, mentorship pairings—that immerse recruits in SOPs from day one. Cap onboarding with mastery assessments to verify comprehension.

4. **Regular Process Audits**
   Machiavelli warns princes against complacency in governance. Similarly, schedule periodic audits—quarterly or biannual—where process owners, peers, and external advisors review SOP compliance, effectiveness, and alignment with evolving strategy. Audit findings drive deliberate updates.

5. **Version Control and Change Management**
   Just as constitutions evolve through amendments, SOPs must adapt without sowing confusion. Maintain version histories, highlight changes prominently, and communicate updates through training sessions or "change days" where teams learn new workflows collaboratively.

SOPs as Cultural Artifacts

Beyond operational function, SOPs embody organizational values. A service-oriented SOP might emphasize empathy in customer communications; a product SOP might mandate user-centered design sprints. Machiavelli understood that princes project values through public works and ceremonies; SOPs serve as daily rituals that reinforce cultural identity. When process documentation reflects the company's ethos—be it bias for action, obsession with quality, or disciplined humility—it not only guides behavior but transmits culture to newcomers.

Cultivating Second-Line Leaders and Succession Planning

Machiavelli argues that a ruler's legacy depends on the cultivation of capable successors: "It is the part of a wise prince to choose those who are able to assist him, rather than those who are grateful to him." In entrepreneurial ventures, the "second line" of leaders—department heads, senior managers, project leaders—must be groomed to carry the torch when founders step back or move on. Succession planning is not a contingency for remote eventualities; it is a core leadership development strategy that ensures continuity and sustained performance.

Identifying and Developing High-Potential Talent

1. **Talent Calibration and Assessment**
   Use structured performance frameworks to identify individuals who combine business acumen, cultural alignment, and growth potential. Deploy 360-degree feedback, peer reviews, and situational simulations to gauge leadership readiness.

2. **Individual Development Plans (IDPs)**
   For each high-potential, craft an IDP that maps stretch

assignments, mentorship relationships, formal courses, and experiential rotations. Rotate talent across functions—finance to product, sales to operations—broadening their organizational fluency and network.

3. **Mentorship and Sponsorship**
   Machiavelli lauds princes who surround themselves with wise mentors. Founders and senior executives should mentor identified successors directly, sharing strategic thinking skills, political acumen, and ethical frameworks. Simultaneously, secure outside sponsors—board members or external advisers—who can champion these leaders' development.

4. **Leadership Academies and Workshops**
   Establish internal programs—quarterly leadership retreats, half-day strategy simulations, peer-coaching circles—that immerse second-line leaders in critical conversations: crisis scenarios, competitive gambits, and cultural diplomacy. These programs transmit tacit knowledge that cannot be captured in manuals.

Formal Succession Protocols

When the unexpected occurs—a founder exit, health crisis, or acquisition—the absence of clear succession plans can paralyze an organization. Machiavelli warns princes to "be diligent in preserving good laws, and in reforming evil ones," a call to codify succession protocols before they are needed.

1. **Emergency Interim Succession**
   Document an immediate chain of command: who acts as interim CEO, who chairs the board, and which committees assume critical decisions. Communicate this plan discreetly to the board and senior team so that, when triggered, roles shift seamlessly.

2. **Long-Term Leadership Pipeline**
   Define multi-year milestones for successor readiness. Align performance incentives—equity vesting, promotion timelines—so that potential successors have clear aspirations tied to organizational health metrics.

3. **Board Oversight of Succession**
   The board of directors—like Machiavelli's ideal council of nobles—must own succession planning as a governance priority. Include succession reviews on the annual board calendar, ensuring that external perspective and accountability drive progress.

4. **Cultural Continuity Checks**
   Successors should be evaluated not only on business results but on their fidelity to core values and cultural DNA. Machiavelli prized rulers who "appear compassionate, faithful, humane," reminding us that cultural alignment cements legitimacy more than technical prowess alone.

By institutionalizing leadership development and succession planning, founders ensure that the enterprise endures beyond individual lifespans, preserving both mission and momentum.

Maintaining Flexibility within Structures

A charge leveled against institutionalization is the risk of calcification: once processes, systems, and hierarchies are in place, innovation and adaptability can stall. Machiavelli himself advises that "those princes who have relied entirely on fortune have always fallen" and that effective rulers "adapt to the times." Likewise, successful organizations embed elasticity into their structures—preserving the ability to pivot, experiment, and renew.

Structural Mechanisms for Agile Renewal

1. **Dual Operating Systems**
    Adopt a "core and innovation" architecture: a stable core responsible for mission-critical operations, governed by established processes, alongside a flexible innovation engine—small cross-functional teams empowered to pursue new ideas with lean, separate KPIs. This mirrors Machiavelli's view that a prince must "maintain freedom of action" even within existing frameworks.

2. **Periodic "Re-founding" Workshops**
    At set intervals—annually or biannually—host company-wide workshops to reexamine purpose, strategy, and key processes. Invite every level of the organization to challenge assumptions and propose improvements, then fast-track adoption of the best ideas.

3. **Adaptive Governance Models**
    Rather than a rigid hierarchy, implement rotating

leadership roles for special initiatives. Task forces or "strike teams" form and dissolve around strategic priorities—market entries, major product launches, acquisition integrations—ensuring the organization can mobilize fresh talent without bureaucracy.

4. **Culture of "Constructive Dissent"**
   Machiavelli valued diverse counsel, warning against sycophants who tell princes only what they want to hear. Encourage dissent through structured mechanisms—devil's advocate roles in decision forums, anonymous suggestion channels, and protected safe spaces for airing unconventional ideas.

5. **Investment in "Optionality"**
   Allocate a portion of budget and headcount to exploratory projects, even during core execution peaks. These "option pools" maintain a pipeline of disruptive ideas. When one shows promise, it can quickly receive additional resources; if not, it can be sunset with minimal disruption.

Embedding Renewal in SOPs

Even the most disciplined SOPs can incorporate clauses for scheduled review and reinvention:

- **Sunset Clauses**: Every process document includes an expiration date—after which it requires reaffirmation or revision before remaining active.

- **Process "Red Teams"**: Assign rotating teams to challenge existing workflows, simulating extreme scenarios to test resilience and propose fortifications or redesigns.

- **Continuous Improvement Culture**: Celebrate teams that identify and decommission outdated processes, rewarding those who streamline and simplify as highly as those who launch new capabilities.

By weaving flexibility into the very fabric of structures, organizations avoid the trap of "institutional sclerosis" and ensure that systems serve strategy rather than constrain it.

Conclusion of Chapter 10

Machiavelli's treatise is not a paean to ruthless singular power but a blueprint for building enduring dominions through foresight, adaptation, and judicious governance. For entrepreneurs, the journey from founder-centric spark to process-driven powerhouse demands institutionalization: codifying workflows that survive individual departures, developing second-line leaders who carry forward the vision, and balancing order with adaptability so that the enterprise thrives amid uncertainty. As Machiavelli instructs, "a prince ought to choose wise men… that they may advise him"—and the wisest founders translate that counsel into resilient systems, structures, and cultures that outlast any one person. By institutionalizing success, startups evolve from fragile experiments into lasting principalities of innovation, ready to command markets and shape industries for generations to come.

Chapter 11: Innovation as Renewal

In the ever-shifting landscape of commerce, resting on past laurels invites decay. Machiavelli warns that "there is nothing more difficult to take in hand, more perilous to conduct, or more uncertain in its success, than to take the lead in the introduction of a new order of things." Yet it is precisely this perilous enterprise that distinguishes enduring principalities from fleeting triumphs. For entrepreneurs, innovation is not a one-off breakthrough but a continual process of renewal – breathing fresh life into products, processes, and organizations. In this chapter, we explore four interlocking imperatives of systemic reinvention: avoiding stagnation through relentless improvement, balancing exploitation and exploration in an ambidextrous organization, establishing protected spaces for unencumbered creativity, and harvesting the ingenuity of every contributor through incentives, hackathons, and crowdsourcing.

Avoiding Stagnation: Continuous Product and Process Improvement

Machiavelli understood that even the most formidable fortress requires constant maintenance. He counseled rulers to "vary innovations gradually, so people grow accustomed to them," recognizing that change both stabilizes and invigorates. In a startup, products and processes alike must evolve iteratively – small refinements aggregating into sustained advantage.

Embracing the Kaizen Mindset

Continuous improvement, or kaizen, demands a culture where every team member feels empowered to suggest refinements. Rather than periodic "big bangs," improvements flow through daily rituals:

- **Daily Stand-Up Retrospectives**: At the close of each stand-up, teams voice one small change they would make to yesterday's workflow or code review process. Over time, these micro-adjustments accelerate throughput and reduce defects.

- **Weekly "Improvement Tickets"**: In the sprint backlog, reserve slots for "technical debt" and "process debt." Engineers and operators convert friction points—broken tests, slow deployments, manual handoffs—into tickets with clear acceptance criteria.

- **Monthly Collective Debriefs**: Cross-functional huddles review aggregated metrics—cycle time, customer satisfaction, error rates—and decide which improvement tickets deserve priority. Machiavelli applauds rulers who examine "the condition of affairs" regularly; startups benefit from the same fiscal honesty.

Embedding Feedback in Every Layer

Machiavelli lauds princes who maintain close counsel and "know the disposition of their troops." In modern terms, that means building true end-to-end feedback loops:

- **In-App Feedback Widgets**: Embed prompts inside your product asking users to rate features or suggest improvements in context, eliminating the friction of separate surveys.

- **Customer Support "Voice of the Customer" Sessions**: Quarterly roundtables where support agents share the top five customer complaints and improvement ideas directly with product and engineering leadership.

- **Automated Process Health Checks**: Build tooling that flags atypical process latencies—code reviews taking more than 48 hours, or failed build rates spiking—to surface issues before they cascade.

By weaving feedback mechanisms throughout the organization, you institutionalize vigilance against stagnation, ensuring that no flaw, however minor, festers unaddressed.

Balancing Exploitation and Exploration: The Ambidextrous Organization

Machiavelli's ideal prince neither clings rigidly to tradition nor plunges recklessly into novelty; he masters both the stability of tradition and the dynamism of change. For startups, this duality manifests as the tension between exploitation—maximizing returns from proven products—and exploration—investigating new opportunities that may fuel future growth.

Dual-Track Structures

An ambidextrous organization explicitly segments teams by orientation:

1. **Exploitation Teams** focus on core products and markets. Their mission is to refine features, optimize conversion funnels, and squeeze incremental gains. They live by metrics—revenue per user, churn rate, operational efficiency—and pursue aggressive continuous improvement.

2. **Exploration Teams** operate in ventures or research labs, with mandates to prototype radical concepts, validate new business models, or test emerging technologies. They measure success by learning velocity: the rate at which experiments yield actionable insight.

Machiavelli would recognize this as akin to maintaining both standing armies for immediate defense and engineering corps for siegecraft and innovation.

Governance and Resource Allocation

To prevent one mode cannibalizing the other, governance must explicitly allocate resources:

- **Budget Pools**: Assign fixed percentages of revenue or investment capital to exploration budgets, immune to periodic cuts when exploitation targets loom large.

- **Board Oversight**: Elevate ambidexterity to the board's agenda. Quarterly, the board reviews both exploitation KPIs and exploration pipelines, ensuring neither starves the other.

- **Innovation Metrics**: Exploration teams track hypothesis-success rates, time to first user feedback, and pivot frequency. If an experiment stalls after multiple iterations, resources are reallocated in a disciplined "fail fast, reallocate faster" process.

Such structural commitment ensures that short-term performance pressures do not throttle long-term renewal.

Setting Up Innovation Labs and "Skunkworks" Teams

Machiavelli admired Cesare Borgia's "spirit of enterprise" in reshaping the Romagna; similarly, modern founders create innovation labs and skunkworks teams—protected enclaves where creative ventures thrive free from the tyranny of incumbency.

Defining the Innovation Charter

An innovation lab requires a clear mandate:

1. **Strategic Horizon**: Specify whether the lab pursues adjacent innovations (new features for existing markets),

transformational innovations (new business models), or entirely speculative breakthroughs (moonshot R&D).

2. **Autonomy Boundaries**: Grant lab teams freedom from corporate bureaucracy—waiving certain approval gates or permitting flexible decision rights—while embedding them within the strategic framework to prevent mission drift.

3. **Success Criteria**: Articulate what validates an idea: technical feasibility demonstration, a minimum viable product with X pilot users, or a partnership with a strategic ally.

Machiavelli would appreciate that a prince "must introduce new orders and modes" through specially designed institutions; the innovation lab is the modern equivalent.

Physical and Psychological Separation

To foster creativity, skunkworks teams need both physical and cultural separation:

- **Physical Space**: Locate the lab in a distinct environment—offsite facility, dedicated wing, or virtual enclave—where norms differ. Walls are painted creatively; open whiteboards teem with sketches; resources for rapid prototyping proliferate.

- **Dedicated Tools**: Provide isolated development environments, CI/CD pipelines, and budget authority for external services, avoiding the slow cadence of shared corporate platforms.

- **Cultural Freedom**: Allow the lab to adopt different operating habits—shorter sprint cycles, alternative design thinking workshops, or non-hierarchical decision forums—while formally extending corporate values of integrity and customer obsession.

This separation echoes Machiavelli's counsel that new institutions require protection from entrenched interests that might undermine them.

Integration Pathways

When prototypes mature, seamless integration with the core business is vital:

- **Hand-Off Protocols**: Define criteria for transitioning mature concepts back to exploitation teams—or spinning them off as independent ventures. Clear guardrails prevent orphaned projects.

- **Leadership Liaisons**: Appoint "innovation ambassadors" on the core product team who maintain daily contact with the skunkworks, ensuring knowledge transfer and technical compatibility.

- **Pilots and Rollouts**: Use the lab to conduct field pilots with select customers, then coordinate with sales, marketing, and support functions for full launch once validated.

By structuring both freedom and integration, founders extract maximum creative output without fracturing the enterprise.

Harvesting Ideas: Incentives, Hackathons, and Crowdsourcing

Even the most promising skunkworks cannot capture all the ingenuity that resides within an organization—or its broader community. Machiavelli emphasizes that "men are so simple and so much creatures of circumstance that the deceiver will always find someone ready to be deceived." In parallel, entrepreneurs must recognize that brilliant ideas can emerge from unexpected quarters; to harness them, they deploy incentives, hackathons, and crowdsourcing as systematic idea-harvesting mechanisms.

Incentive Programs for Intrapreneurship

Aligning individual motivation with organizational renewal requires carefully designed incentive schemes:

- **Innovation Bonuses and Grants**: Allocate a fund for "innovation grants" that individuals or teams can apply to pursue side projects. Successful prototypes may receive additional resources or equity-linked bonuses.

- **Equity "Idea Shares"**: When employees propose ideas that lead to new product lines or feature sets generating revenue, grant them a percentage of the incremental profits—mirroring the Machiavellian logic of rewarding loyal subjects who serve the prince's ambitions.

- **Public Recognition**: Celebrate "innovator of the month" at all-hands meetings, documenting accomplishments on company intranets. Machiavelli recognized the power of pageantry; public recognition cements behavior as valued.

Hackathons and Innovation Sprints

Time-boxed, event-based competitions channel collective creativity:

1. **Theme Selection**: Anchor each hackathon around strategic themes—improving onboarding, sustainability solutions, AI-powered workflows—ensuring ideas align with business priorities.

2. **Cross-Functional Teams**: Mix engineers, designers, marketers, and even customer-support reps to foster cross-pollination. Diversity amplifies problem-solving power.

3. **Rapid Prototyping Support**: Provide toolkits—APIs, data sandboxes, design libraries—and mentors to guide technical and customer-validation challenges.

4. **Judging and Follow-Up**: Executive panels evaluate hackathon outputs, selecting winners for further incubation. Runners-up receive "innovation flex" time to refine

concepts.

Machiavelli admired those who acted quickly—"injury must be done all at once"—and hackathons compress ideation and execution into a surge, rapidly exposing promising concepts.

Crowdsourcing Beyond the Firewall

Open innovation invites external contributors – customers, partners, and enthusiasts – into the creative fold:

- **Idea Portals**: Public platforms where users submit feature requests, vote on proposals, and collaborate on specification documents. Transparent roadmaps incorporate top-voted ideas, validating customer priorities.

- **Partner Co-Development**: Joint programs with key customers or suppliers to co-design specialized solutions. Machiavelli would liken this to treaty-bound alliances, where shared endeavors bind parties more tightly.

- **Developer Ecosystems**: For software platforms, provide comprehensive SDKs, documentation, and marketplaces enabling third-party developers to build extensions. This multiplies your innovation capacity far beyond in-house limits.

Crowdsourcing transforms passive consumers into active co-creators, expanding the frontiers of possibility.

Conclusion

Innovation is the lifeblood that renews entrepreneurial principalities, enabling them to withstand the caprices of fortune and the assaults of fierce rivals. Machiavelli's timeless counsel—that new orders must be introduced with daring, guided by prudence, and protected by wise institutions—illuminates the path. By embedding continuous product and process improvements, balancing exploitation with exploration in ambidextrous structures, erecting innovation labs and skunkworks enclaves, and harvesting the collective ingenuity of employees and communities through incentives, hackathons, and crowdsourcing, founders construct an ever-evolving fortress. In so doing, they ensure that every conquest is but a stepping stone to the next, and that their enterprises remain vibrant, adaptive, and impervious to stagnation. As Machiavelli might conclude, "for a prince, nothing is more important than the foundations of his state," and for the modern entrepreneur, nothing is more vital than the structures of renewal that undergird lasting success.

Chapter 12: Risk, Reputation, and Resilience

Even the most formidable principality, having expanded through shrewd alliances and relentless innovation, remains vulnerable to forces beyond its control. Machiavelli reminds us that "fortune is the ruler of one-half of our actions, but that she still leaves us the freedom to direct the other half." To thrive amid black swans and shocks, founders must build resilience into every facet of their enterprises—anticipating crises, safeguarding reputation when errors occur, stockpiling buffers to absorb shocks, and cultivating a Machiavellian mindset that meets adversity head-on.

Preparing for Black Swan Events and Market Shocks

Black swan events—rare, unforeseen, and immensely impactful—can upend entire industries overnight. From a global pandemic to a sudden regulatory clampdown, these shocks expose enterprises whose risk management was superficial, revealing brittle strategies and overextended positions. Machiavelli warns that "he who neglects what is at hand and looks to what is afar off will soon fall," urging leaders to scan the horizon without ignoring present vulnerabilities.

Stress-Testing Your Business Model

1. **Scenario Planning Workshops**
    Convene cross-functional teams—product, finance, operations, legal—to map extreme but plausible scenarios. What if revenue drops 50 percent in a month? What if a key supplier collapses? What if customer data is exposed? For each scenario, document chain reactions across P&L, cash flow, and customer experience.

2. **"Red Team" and "Blue Team" Exercises**
    Borrowing from military wargaming, appoint a "red team" to play adversarial roles—regulators, competitors, insider threats—while the "blue team" defends. These exercises uncover blind spots in crisis protocols and reveal assumptions that crumble under pressure.

3. **Reverse Stress Tests**
    Instead of asking "what could go wrong?", ask "what conditions would force us into insolvency or catastrophic failure?" Work backward to identify the threshold events—mass customer churn, 80 percent supply-chain disruption, decisive legal rulings—that trigger existential risk.

4. **Early-Warning Indicators**
    For each critical vulnerability, define leading indicators: social-media sentiment dips that presage reputational hits, inventory-to-sales ratios signaling supply issues, cash runway falling below six months. Automate dashboards that flash alerts when indicators cross risk thresholds, ensuring leadership can intervene before crises cascade.

Diversification and Optionality

Machiavelli warns princes against relying on mercenary armies; similarly, over-dependence on a single market, supplier, or business line invites disaster. Build optionality by:

- **Geographic Spread:** Enter multiple regions or channels so that a localized shock—natural disaster, political unrest, regional regulation—only dents, but does not decapitate, revenues.

- **Product and Revenue Diversification:** Cultivate adjacent revenue streams—consulting, services, subscription tiers—that can be scaled up if core offerings falter.

- **Supply-Chain Redundancy:** Qualify secondary suppliers in different geographies; pre-negotiate safety-stock agreements so you can pivot when primary sources fail.

This layered defense parallels Machiavelli's advice that a prince fortify both city walls and countryside strongholds, ensuring that if one barrier falls, others hold.

Building a Crisis Response Operating System

A principality caught unprepared for siege finds its defenses overwhelmed; enterprises without a crisis OS descend into chaos when shocks arrive. Essential elements include:

1. **Crisis Charter and Governance:** Define who sits on the Crisis Management Team (CMT)—CEO, COO, CFO, head

of communications, legal counsel—and document decision-rights, meeting cadence, and escalation protocols.

2. **Communication Protocols:** Develop pre-approved templates for internal alerts (staff email, intranet posts), customer advisories (service-status pages, direct emails), and media statements. Clarity and speed forestall rumor mills and speculation.

3. **Decision-Rights Matrix:** In different crisis phases—initial triage, stabilization, recovery—assign decision authority to the appropriate role. Early tactical fixes may rest with functional heads; strategic pivots fall to the CMT.

4. **Simulation Drills:** Just as armies rehearse battle plans, run quarterly crisis simulations—with injects like cyber attacks or regulatory subpoenas—to stress capability and refine procedures.

By institutionalizing crisis readiness, founders convert reactive firefighting into practiced maneuvers, ensuring that disruptive events trigger protocols rather than panic.

Reputation Management: Recovering from Missteps

Reputation is the currency of trust; it takes years to build and can be shattered in hours. Machiavelli teaches that "men judge generally more by the eye than by the hand"—perception outweighs reality. When missteps occur—product failures, data breaches, executive scandals—how a leader responds often cements or erodes long-term legitimacy.

Acknowledge Swiftly, Empathize Genuinely

Silence or obfuscation deepens distrust. In the immediate aftermath of any misstep:

1. **Prompt Public Acknowledgment:** Issue a clear statement admitting the issue, outlining its scope, and committing to rigorous investigation. Delay only fuels speculation and conspiracies.

2. **Express Genuine Empathy:** Speak to affected stakeholders—customers, employees, partners—with authentic regret for their disruption or harm. Machiavelli might note that a prince who displays measured compassion secures loyalty; entrepreneurs who humanize mistakes retain goodwill.

3. **Transparent Roadmap to Resolution:** Share tangible next steps—bug fixes, service credits, leadership changes—with estimated timelines. Provide regular status updates, even if incremental, reinforcing that the

organization remains accountable.

Engage Affected Communities

When reputation stumbles, the court extends beyond customers: employees, regulators, investors, and social-media communities all weigh in. To repair trust:

- **Customer Town Halls and Webinars:** Host live Q&A sessions with executives, acknowledging concerns and detailing corrective measures. Personal interaction quells frustration more effectively than emailed communiqués.

- **Employee Forums:** Bring the team into the remedy process—invite them to submit improvement ideas, serve as ambassadors in communications, and reinforce shared purpose. Studies show that employees who feel part of the fix become your best advocates.

- **Regulatory Cooperation:** If a breach involves legal or compliance lapses, proactively engage regulators, share investigation findings, and demonstrate enhancements to controls. This pre-empts punitive actions and signals seriousness.

Reframing Through Action

Machiavelli extols rulers who, after quashing rebellion, enact benevolent public works to renew popular affection. Similarly, after crisis resolution:

1. **Overdeliver on Promises:** If you pledged feature enhancements or security upgrades, execute them with urgency and exceed baseline expectations.

2. **Publicize Learnings:** Publish a "lessons learned" white paper or blog series explaining root causes and preventive measures. This reframes the misstep as an impetus for institutional strengthening.

3. **Invest in Reputation-Enhancing Initiatives:** Launch customer-centric programs—extended warranties, free training, community grants—that demonstrate commitment to stakeholder success, counterbalancing the sting of the error.

Reputation recovery is neither quick nor linear, but with deliberate transparency, empathy, and over-performance, leaders can transform scars into badges of reliability.

Building Financial and Operational Buffers

In Machiavelli's time, a principality's endurance depended on granaries to withstand famine and treasuries to fund defense. For startups, financial and operational buffers serve equivalent functions—absorbing shocks, enabling counter-moves, and preserving options when revenues ebb or crises strike.

Financial Reserves: Rainy-Day Capital

1. **Cash Runway Targets:** Rather than extend runway until the last possible month before insolvency, adopt a policy of maintaining at least 12–18 months of operating expenses in cash or liquid equivalents. Machiavelli would commend prudence: "He who is overly generous rests on uncertain foundations."

2. **Capital Facility Lines:** Negotiate undrawn credit facilities—venture debt lines, revolvers—with banks or specialized lenders when your balance sheet is strong. These standby lines provide immediate liquidity without dilutive equity.

3. **Dynamic Cash-Flow Modeling:** Move beyond static budgets; build rolling 18-month forecasts updated monthly to capture new hires, seasonality, and capital expenditures. Embed trigger points—if cash dips below nine months' runway, pause nonessential spending.

Operational Slack: Flex-Capacity and Redundancy

1. **Flexible Workforce Models:** Combine full-time teams with vetted contractors and on-demand specialist networks. During downturns, adjustable staffing levels reduce fixed-cost burdens without wholesale layoffs.

2. **Modular Infrastructure:** Use cloud services and containerized deployments that can scale compute and storage up or down. Avoid large upfront investments in on-premises hardware that become stranded assets when

demand contracts.

3. **Cross-Training and Role Redundancy:** Train individuals to cover critical functions—accounting, DevOps, customer support—so that departures or spikes in demand do not incapacitate the organization. Machiavelli recognized the danger when power resided in a single advisor; spreading capability prevents single points of failure.

Strategic Inventory and Supply-Chain Buffers

In product-oriented ventures:

- **Safety Stock Policies:** Determine optimal inventory buffers based on supply-chain variability and demand volatility, balancing carrying costs against stock-out risks.

- **Multi-Tier Vendor Strategies:** Qualify both Tier-1 and Tier-2 suppliers, keeping contracts with staggered lead times so you can shift orders swiftly when primary sources falter.

- **Demand-Driven Replenishment:** Use real-time sales and usage data to trigger automated reordering, minimizing overstock while ensuring continuity.

By embedding financial and operational slack, enterprises transform the capricious gusts of market turbulence into manageable headwinds rather than crushing storms.

The "Machiavellian" Mindset in Crisis Leadership

Finally, beyond systems and buffers, resilience emerges from a leader's mindset. Machiavelli's ideal prince combines cunning foresight with resolute action—"like the fox and the lion"—guarding against unseen snares while wielding strength where needed. For founders, this mindset translates into four interlocking disciplines:

1. **Calculated Boldness**
   In crisis, fainthearted caution cedes initiative to competitors. Machiavelli teaches that "fortune favors the bold." Leaders must weigh risks swiftly, commit to decisive courses—whether shoring up core offerings, pivoting business models, or securing bridge financing—and embrace temporary discomfort for long-term survival.

2. **Emotional Equanimity**
   Crises amplify emotions—panic, guilt, anger. The Machiavellian prince remains composed, issuing calm directives that instill confidence. Practices such as pausing before major announcements, rehearsing key messages, and housing crisis teams in secure war rooms reduce emotional contagion and maintain clear heads.

3. **Relentless Curiosity**
   Every shock reveals latent vulnerabilities and hidden opportunities. A Machiavellian founder interrogates root causes with ruthless curiosity: Why did the system fail?

Which customers left and why? Which parts of the business thrived under pressure? This diagnostic rigor fuels both recovery and reinvention.

4. **Moral Pragmatism**
   While Machiavelli is associated with ruthless cunning, he affirms that excessive cruelty breeds hatred, which undermines rule. Founders must balance tough decisions—staff reductions, price hikes, partner exits—with humane treatment and transparent rationale. This moral pragmatism preserves the loyalty and respect critical for collective resilience.

Conclusion of Chapter 12

In the interplay of risk, reputation, and resilience, Machiavelli's enduring wisdom equips modern entrepreneurs to navigate crises with foresight, resolve, and integrity. By preparing for black swan events through scenario planning and optionality, managing reputation with transparency and empathy, building robust financial and operational buffers, and embodying a Machiavellian mindset of bold equanimity and pragmatic ethics, founders transform peril into potential. The principalities they build do not merely survive tumult; they harness upheaval as forge-fires that temper their strengths, sharpen their strategies, and cement their rule in the marketplace for years to come.

Chapter 13: Expansion and Diversification

Having forged a resilient principality through disciplined governance, strategic alliances, and relentless innovation, a mature venture faces its next challenge: extending its dominion without overreach. Machiavelli instructs that "it must be remembered that there is nothing more difficult to plan, more doubtful of success, nor more dangerous to manage than the creation of a new order of things." Expansion and diversification represent a new order—one that offers fresh opportunity but carries acute risks. In this chapter, we explore four interrelated dimensions of growth strategy: choosing between horizontal and vertical expansion; entering new markets with rigorous due diligence and local adaptation; executing mergers and acquisitions with integration finesse; and discerning when to spin off, license, or divest business units.

Horizontal vs. Vertical Growth Strategies

Machiavelli's prince who seeks to safeguard his realm weighs the benefits of annexing neighboring territories against the burdens of governing distant lands. Entrepreneurs confront a similar choice: should they widen their product portfolio to adjacent offerings (horizontal growth), or deepen their control over the value chain (vertical growth)?

Horizontal Expansion: Broadening the Offering

Horizontal growth entails adding new products or services that appeal to existing customers. A software firm might introduce complementary modules; a consumer brand might launch new flavors or sub-brands. The strategic appeal lies in:

- **Leveraging Brand Equity:** Existing goodwill and brand recognition reduce the friction of customer acquisition for new offerings.

- **Economies of Scope:** Shared marketing channels, sales teams, and customer-support infrastructure lower incremental costs.

- **Risk Diversification:** If demand for one product softens, alternate lines cushion revenue streams.

Yet horizontal moves can stretch organizational focus. Machiavelli cautions that a ruler who "extends his conquests in too many directions leaves each without sufficient garrison." In business terms, spreading R&D, marketing, and distribution effort across too many offerings can dilute quality, confuse the brand, and overwhelm support functions. To succeed:

1. **Customer-Centric Ideation:** Solicit direct feedback from your core user base to identify adjacent needs that they prize most. Prioritize those with high willingness to pay and minimal cannibalization of existing lines.

2. **Pilot and Learn:** Launch new products to a select
    segment or geography, rigorously measuring uptake,
    retention, and cross-sell uplift before committing broad
    resources.

3. **Modular Architecture:** Design products with shared
    platforms—APIs, design systems, data models—so
    horizontal expansion requires minimal retooling. This
    mirrors Machiavelli's advice that new institutions should
    build on existing foundations rather than erect entirely
    novel structures.

Vertical Expansion: Controlling the Value Chain

Vertical growth entails extending upstream (toward suppliers) or
downstream (toward customers) along the industry value chain. A
manufacturer might acquire a raw-material plant (backward
integration), or a retailer might open proprietary factories (forward
integration). Vertical moves can yield:

- **Margin Capture:** By internalizing formerly external
  markups, firms boost profitability.

- **Supply Reliability:** Owners of critical inputs can insulate
  against supplier disruptions and price volatility.

- **Customer Lock-In:** End-to-end control over production
  and distribution can create seamless, differentiated
  experiences.

Yet vertical integration demands new capabilities. Machiavelli warns that "mercenary troops… are dangerous and despised because they are disunited," implying that adding unfamiliar functions without cohesive culture and expertise invites fracturing. To mitigate this:

1. **Capability Assessment:** Rigorously analyze whether you possess—or can feasibly acquire—the operational skills, capital intensity, and regulatory acumen needed for integration.

2. **Strategic Partnerships as Stepping Stones:** Consider joint ventures or minority stakes in supplier or distribution partners before full acquisition, testing the water for integration synergies without full commitment.

3. **Cultural Alignment and Change Management:** New functions must embrace the existing organizational ethos. Machiavelli would counsel the prince to "preserve the good laws of the old state" when establishing new officeholders; similarly, integration teams must be inducted into core values and management rhythms.

Choosing the Right Path

The horizontal–vertical decision is not binary; sophisticated enterprises often pursue a hybrid, horizontal moves today, vertical tomorrow, guided by clear capital-allocation frameworks. Machiavelli's overarching lesson—that "fortune favors the bold" when backed by prudence—applies: choose the path whose rewards exceed execution risk given your unique strengths.

Entering New Markets: Due Diligence and Local Adaptation

Conquest of distant lands in Machiavelli's Italy required careful study of local customs, alliances with influential families, and judicious imposition of laws. Similarly, geographic or demographic market entry demands rigorous due diligence and deep local adaptation to avoid costly missteps.

Market Due Diligence: Mapping the Terrain

Before planting your banner, conduct thorough "market intelligence":

1. **Regulatory Landscape:** Catalog licensing requirements, trade barriers, tax regimes, labor laws, and data-privacy statutes. In regulated domains—healthcare, finance, energy—noncompliance imposes existential risk.

2. **Competitive Field Survey:** Identify incumbent strengths, substitute offerings, price structures, and potential partners or adversaries. An aggressive competitor may trigger a defensive entrenchment rather than entry.

3. **Customer Behavior and Preferences:** Through primary research—surveys, focus groups, ethnographic observation—understand how local consumers differ in language, cultural norms, buying triggers, and brand

perceptions.

4. **Distribution and Channel Analysis:** Map existing distribution networks—retail partners, digital platforms, logistics providers—to gauge ease of access and potential bottlenecks in getting the product to market.

Machiavelli would applaud the prince who "conducts himself in such a manner that, when his deeds are reported, they excite wonder and admiration." In business, a meticulously prepared market-entry strategy impresses stakeholders and reduces surprise.

Local Adaptation: Respecting the Customs

Even with solid due diligence, formulas that succeeded at home often stumble abroad if transplanted rigidly. To adapt:

1. **Product Localization:** Beyond language translation, tailor features, packaging, and pricing to local tastes and purchasing power. A Machiavellian ruler would show reverence for local traditions to win hearts; entrepreneurs must show respect for local consumer mores.

2. **Go-To-Market Customization:** Marketing messages must resonate culturally—leveraging local influencers, narratives, and holidays. A campaign that references local idioms and symbols signals genuine investment rather than opportunistic transplantation.

3. **Partnership with Local Allies:** Forge alliances with respected local distributors, joint-venture partners, or licensing agents. Machiavelli extols alliances with influential families; modern counterparts are channel partners who command relationships with end customers.

4. **Organizational Presence and Governance:** Establish a local leadership team with native expertise, empowered with decision-rights rather than micromanaged remotely. This autonomy ensures swift adaptation to unfolding realities.

Portfolio Approach to Market Entry

To manage risk, leading firms use a staged portfolio approach:

- **Greenfield Pilots:** Launch small-scale, company-owned pilots to trial assumptions.

- **Franchise or Licensing Models:** Where brand equity matters but capital commitment is constrained, license local operators under strict brand and quality guidelines.

- **Acquisition of Local Players:** In some cases, acquiring a well-established local firm provides instant scale and market know-how—though integration challenges loom.

Machiavelli taught that "a wise prince ought to follow that course which is most useful," reminding entrepreneurs to align entry modes with strategic and financial realities.

Mergers and Acquisitions: Integration Challenges and Tactics

When conquering new dominions, princes often absorbed rival states through marriage pacts or outright force. In business, mergers and acquisitions offer a rapid route to scale, capabilities, or market access—but integration missteps can squander value.

Pre-Deal Strategic Clarity

Before signing any letter of intent, define:

1. **Strategic Rationale:** Is the acquisition about market access, technology acquisition, talent, or eliminating competition? Ambiguous motives lead to confused integration priorities.

2. **Value Creation Plan:** Quantify expected synergies—cost savings, cross-sell revenue, R&D acceleration—and map who is responsible for each target. Machiavelli would note that "it is not titles that honor men, but men that honor titles"; similarly, clear accountability honors the strategic ambition.

3. **Integration Risk Assessment:** Evaluate cultural compatibility, systems heterogeneity, regulatory hurdles, and retention risks. Use this to calibrate purchase price and structure earn-outs or holdbacks.

Integration Tactics: From "Day One" to "Day One Hundred"

1. **Integration Management Office (IMO):** Stand up a cross-functional team—led by a seasoned integration manager—tasked with orchestrating the move. Like a prince's war council, the IMO directs specialized squads: technology, HR, operations, sales, and communications.

2. **"100-Day Plan":** Define critical milestones for the first three months post-close—employee communications, system cutovers, initial synergies captured. Publish this plan to leadership and key stakeholders to align focus.

3. **Cultural Integration Roadmap:** Conduct joint workshops and town halls to articulate a unified mission, address anxieties, and celebrate combined strengths. Machiavelli recognized that subjects rally around symbols; a shared narrative and emblem reinforce unity.

4. **Systems and Process Harmonization:** Inventory all key systems—ERP, CRM, auditing—and decide quickly which to retire, replace, or interconnect. Prolonged dual-system operations breed errors and complexity.

5. **Talent Retention Strategies:** Identify "critical contributors" whose departure would imperil value capture. Offer retention bonuses, new career paths, and inclusion in leadership forums to secure their commitment.

Avoiding the "Acquisition Trap"

Machiavelli warns against overextension: "A prince who builds nothing but relies on the labor of others builds fragile foundations." Acquisitions financed by excessive leverage can erode balance sheets and distract management. To avoid this:

- **Disciplined Pricing:** Cap bid prices based on conservative synergy assumptions; walk away if seller expectations exceed your valuation comfort zone.

- **Modular Integration:** Instead of full absorption, consider maintaining the acquired entity as an independent subsidiary until integration delivers track record results, then proceed further.

- **Post-Mortem Reviews:** After each acquisition, perform an honest "lessons learned" analysis—what worked, what didn't—and refine governance for future deals.

Through rigorous planning, decisive execution, and reflective learning, mergers and acquisitions can become potent catalysts rather than costly detours.

When to Spin Off, License, or Divest

Just as principalities fracture when princes fail to cede distant outposts they cannot defend, companies that cling to non-core or underperforming units drain resources and focus. Machiavelli counsels that "he who becomes prince through the favor of the people ought to commit no act that will alienate their affections," reminding leaders that strategic withdrawal, when communicated effectively, preserves goodwill and redirects energy where it matters most.

Spin-Offs: Unlocking Independent Value

Spinning off divisions into standalone companies can generate value by granting them strategic autonomy and tailored capital structures. Ideal candidates:

- **High-Growth Niches:** Units whose growth trajectories and capital needs diverge sharply from the core business—e.g., a legacy hardware division versus a cloud-native SaaS arm.

- **Distinct Cultures:** Teams that operate with different risk profiles, sales motions, or regulatory demands.

- **Market Signaling:** Spin-offs often trade at higher multiples than conglomerates, unlocking hidden equity value.

Successful spin-offs require:

1. **Robust Corporate Separation Plan:** Define legal, financial, operational, and human-resource disentanglement steps, ensuring smooth continued operations.

2. **Dedicated Leadership and Governance:** Appoint experienced management teams and independent boards for the spun entity. Machiavelli praised princes who installed loyal yet competent governors in new lands.

3. **Brand Strategies:** Decide whether the spin-off retains elements of the parent brand or forges a new identity—balancing customer familiarity against the need to craft a distinct value proposition.

Licensing: Monetizing Intellectual Property

When direct operation is suboptimal, licensing technology, brands, or processes to partners can generate recurring royalties with minimal capital investment. Licensing suits:

- **Geographies Beyond Core Markets:** Local licensees bear market-entry risks while you collect fees.

- **Non-Core Applications:** When your IP has applications outside your strategic focus—e.g., a diagnostic algorithm licensed to veterinary or agricultural use.

- **Fragmented Markets:** Industries where partnering with multiple licensees yields broad coverage without building direct sales teams.

Key licensing best practices:

- **Precise Agreement Drafting:** Define scope, territories, permitted applications, and quality standards to protect brand and IP integrity.

- **Ongoing Compliance Audits:** Periodic reviews ensure licensees adhere to guidelines; Machiavelli valued vigilant oversight to prevent subversive behavior.

- **Incentivized Royalty Structures:** Graduated royalty rates reward volume or performance, aligning licensee ambition with your returns.

Divestitures: Cutting Losses and Refocusing

When a business unit consistently underperforms, or when strategic priorities shift, divestiture may be the best path. Though painful, divestitures free up capital and management bandwidth. Execution considerations:

1. **Valuation Realism:** Use normalized earnings and divestiture comps to set price expectations. Machiavelli would advise against overreliance on optimistic forecasts that sour negotiations.

2. **Stakeholder Communication:** Transparently explain the rationale—focus on core strengths, reallocate resources to higher-return areas—to employees, investors, and customers, mitigating uncertainty.

3. **Transition Services Agreements (TSAs):** Provide temporary shared services—IT, HR, finance—for a defined

period to ensure continuity, but cap TSA durations to avoid extended entanglement.

4. **Reinvestment Strategy:** Immediately redeploy divestiture proceeds into strategic priorities—R&D, geographic expansion, debt reduction—to signal disciplined capital management.

Through timely spin-offs, licensing, and divestitures, entrepreneurs sculpt their portfolios, concentrating on domains where they possess unique advantage and shedding distractions that erode performance.

Conclusion of Chapter 13

Expansion and diversification, like military campaigns beyond a principality's core territory, demand bold vision tempered by rigorous planning and disciplined execution. Machiavelli's wisdom resounds: "One change always leaves the way open for the establishment of others." By choosing between horizontal and vertical growth aligned with organizational strengths; conducting meticulous due diligence and adapting to local nuances when entering new markets; structuring mergers and acquisitions for seamless integration; and deploying spin-offs, licensing, or divestitures to refine the portfolio, founders extend their dominions thoughtfully. In so doing, they transform episodic triumphs into enduring empires—enterprises agile enough to seize new frontiers and resilient enough to govern them well.

Chapter 14: Legacy and Exit

As every principality must eventually reckon with the passage of its founding ruler, so every entrepreneurial journey confronts the question of legacy and exit. Machiavelli reminds us that "a prince ought to desire to be honored and esteemed," yet also warns that "his glory must endure beyond his life." For founders, crafting a legacy and orchestrating an exit demands the same strategic acumen that guided their ventures from inception to maturity. In this final chapter, we explore four interwoven dimensions of this culminating phase: defining your entrepreneurial legacy; timing and structuring the optimal exit—whether IPO, sale, or handover; reimagining your own identity post-exit; and extending your influence through philanthropy, mentorship, and enduring impact.

Defining Your Entrepreneurial Legacy

Long before the moment of departure arrives, a wise founder contemplates the story that will outlive them. Machiavelli counsels that "one change always leaves the way open for the establishment of others," underscoring how each leader's actions embed precedents into the fabric of the state. Similarly, every strategic choice, cultural value, and public statement contributes to the narrative tapestry woven around a founder's name.

Articulating Your Core Values

Your legacy begins with the principles that guided every decision:

- **Visionary Ambition:** Did you pioneer a new market category or redefine industry norms?

- **Cultural DNA:** What core behaviors—relentless customer obsession, empirical rigor, radical collaboration—became non-negotiable?

- **Ethical Compass:** How did you balance ruthless competition with integrity and respect for stakeholders?

By distilling these into a concise "Founder's Manifesto," you create a charter that will anchor the organization's ethos long after your departure.

Monumental Achievements vs. Everyday Impact

Machiavelli admired princes who left behind grand public works—bridges, fortifications, institutions—that symbolized their reign. Yet he also recognized the power of intangible legacies: the loyalty of troops, the memory of decisive victories. Founders, too, build legacies on two levels:

1. **Crown Jewels:** Landmark achievements—groundbreaking products, record-breaking revenues, transformative mergers—that mark definitive turning points in your industry.

2. **Bedrock Practices:** The small but persistent rituals—weekly town halls, "failure postmortems," transparent OKR tracking—that shaped how people work,

learn, and collaborate.

A balanced legacy celebrates both the zenith moments and the everyday disciplines that collectively forged enduring success.

Inscribing Your Story

How will future generations recount your tenure? Machiavelli stresses the importance of controlling the narrative: "it is better to be impetuous than cautious, for fortune is a woman." Founders can shape their biography through:

- **Memoirs and Thought Leadership:** Publishing candid accounts of both triumphs and setbacks cements lessons learned while humanizing the founder's journey.

- **Corporate Histories and Archives:** Commission a formal history—videos, written chronicles, timelines—that documents pivotal events, decisions, and personalities.

- **Named Endowments and Buildings:** Whether a research institute, an innovation center, or a scholarship fund, attaching your name to physical institutions perpetuates remembrance.

By proactively inscribing your story, you ensure that posterity views your legacy through the lens you intended.

Timing and Structuring an Exit: IPO, Sale, or Handover

When to relinquish control, and how to do so smoothly, are questions laden with strategic nuance. Machiavelli advises that "a wise prince never occupies himself entirely with either affairs; he devotes part of his attention to them both," suggesting that even in moments of transition, leaders balance the demands of current rule with planning for succession. Founders must choose the exit route—public offering, strategic sale, or internal handover—that best aligns with their objectives and the venture's health.

Initial Public Offering (IPO)

An IPO offers founders the opportunity to monetize equity, gain public visibility, and create a currency for acquisitions and incentives. Yet it brings regulatory scrutiny, short-term earnings pressures, and loss of privacy.

- **Ideal Conditions:** Strong, predictable growth; robust governance structures; an experienced leadership team; favorable market valuations.

- **Preparation:** Audited financials, seasoned board composition with independent directors, Sarbanes–Oxley–compliant controls, investor relations machinery.

- **Lock-Up and Transition:** Founders typically face a 180-day lock-up on share sales; plot gradual equity liquidation to avoid market flooding while signaling confidence through retained ownership.

Machiavelli would note that public princes must "play to the galleries"—delivering quarterly performances that satisfy public expectations even as they pursue long-term strategy.

Strategic Sale or Merger

Selling to a larger player can accelerate growth, provide resources for global expansion, or simply deliver immediate financial return. But value capture hinges on seamless integration and alignment of cultures.

- **Buyer Selection:** Seek acquirers whose strategic objectives complement yours—market entry, technology synergies, distribution scale—over those driven solely by cost-cutting.

- **Deal Structure:** Balance cash and stock components; negotiate earn-outs tied to retention goals; secure employment or consulting agreements that retain your expertise during transition.

- **Cultural Preservation:** Advocate for carve-outs or semi-autonomous business units to protect your venture's identity within a sprawling conglomerate.

Machiavelli's ideal ruler would counsel founders to "secure the affections of their people by acts of benefaction," meaning that in a sale, preserving your team's morale and the customer experience is paramount.

Handover to Successors

Some founders choose to step aside in favor of internal successors—CEOs groomed over years of shared leadership. This route preserves the venture's independence but requires careful calibration.

- **Succession Planning:** Identify, develop, and empower a second-line leader with proven track record, cultural alignment, and stakeholder confidence.

- **Governance Pact:** Establish a handover charter delineating your continuing role (chairman, executive advisor) versus operational authority, ensuring clarity and minimizing mixed signals.

- **Gradual Transition:** Phase out day-to-day involvement over a predetermined timeline, enabling the successor to build their own credibility while you remain available for counsel.

Machiavelli recognized that "men change princes not because of the goodness of the new, but because of resentment toward the old," teaching founders that exit must minimize friction, honoring both custodianship and renewal.

Hybrid and Alternative Exits

Innovative structures—partial recapitalizations, dual-class share adjustments, or management buyouts—offer nuanced paths that blend liquidity with continued influence. Analyze these options against your personal goals, tax implications, and appetite for involvement.

Personal Reinvention Post-Exit

Stepping away from the helm creates a void that extends beyond professional identity. Machiavelli's exile upon the fall of the Medici court underscores the founder's need for new purpose and self-conception after reign ends. Successful exits entail personal reinvention.

Reflecting on Identity Beyond the Title

Many founders tie self-worth to company performance. Breaking that bond involves:

- **Mindset Shift:** Embrace the notion that your value extends beyond one enterprise. Cultivate interests—writing, teaching, art, philanthropy—that reflect broader passions.

- **Rituals of Closure:** Host a formal farewell—company-wide gatherings, public ceremonies—that ritualizes the end of one chapter and legitimizes the beginning of another. Machiavelli understood the power of ceremony to mark transitions and stabilize followers' morale.

Mapping Your Next Moves

Post-exit life unfolds across several domains:

1. **Portfolio Career:** Advisors, board seats, angel investing allow you to leverage your expertise while maintaining autonomy and variety.

2. **Entrepreneurial Re-Entry:** Some founders launch "founder-in-residence" roles at incubators or start new ventures, applying hard-earned lessons to fresh challenges.

3. **Academic and Thought Leadership:** Fellowships, professorships, and conference circuits position you as an elder statesperson, shaping future innovators.

Set deliberate goals—revenue from advisory practice, number of startups backed, books published—to maintain momentum and avoid drift.

Well-Being and Balance

High-intensity leadership often exacts personal costs. Post-exit reinvention provides an opportunity to recalibrate:

- **Health and Wellness:** Prioritize physical and mental health—exercise regimens, mindfulness practices, therapy. Machiavelli praised rulers who maintained vigor; founders, too, flourish with robust well-being.

- **Family and Relationships:** Reinvest in personal connections neglected during the startup years.

By designing a purposeful, balanced post-exit life, you ensure that your second act resonates with fulfillment and impact.

Philanthropy, Mentorship, and Enduring Influence

As Machiavelli intimates, princes secure their names through public benefactions and monuments that stand as testaments to their reign. For modern founders, philanthropy, mentorship, and thought leadership create living legacies that outlast any corporate structure.

Strategic Philanthropy

Moving beyond ad hoc donations, strategic philanthropy aligns personal passions with systemic change:

- **Theory of Change:** Define the social, environmental, or educational outcomes you seek—closing the STEM achievement gap, advancing renewable energy, supporting underserved entrepreneurs—and allocate resources accordingly.

- **Impact Measurement:** Establish clear metrics—lives improved, emissions reduced, businesses launched—and apply the same rigor to philanthropic programs as to commercial ventures.

- **Collaborative Funds and Foundations:** Partner with NGOs, governments, and community organizations, leveraging co-funding and domain expertise to amplify impact.

Machiavelli notes that "benefits ought to be given little by little, so they may be tasted and enjoyed every day." Consider recurring scholarship awards, grant cycles, or community programs that foster sustained goodwill.

Mentorship and Capacity Building

Your experiences, both triumphant and painful, constitute a rich knowledge base. Structured mentorship magnifies your influence:

- **Mentor Networks:** Join or create programs that match founders with seasoned advisors. Provide not just advice but introductions, credibility, and moral support.

- **Masterclasses and Workshops:** Deliver deep-dive sessions on fundraising, scaling teams, or crisis management—areas where your Machiavellian insights prove most practical.

- **Writing and Speaking:** Publish articles, deliver keynotes, and participate in podcasts to disseminate hard-won lessons to wider audiences.

Through consistent mentorship, you propagate a culture of strategic realism—tempered by integrity—that redefines industry norms.

Thought Leadership and Institutional Roles

To shape systems at scale, assume roles in policy, academia, and industry bodies:

- **Advisory Councils:** Serve on government or nonprofit boards crafting technology, education, or economic policies.

- **Academic Affiliations:** Establish chairs or research centers at leading universities, ensuring that your strategic framework influences curriculum and future leaders.

- **Industry Consortiums:** Lead standard-setting efforts or ethical frameworks—data privacy, AI governance—that codify best practices.

These positions allow you to "choose wise men" around you, extending your principality's values into broader social structures.

Epilogue

Machiavelli closes *The Prince* not with guarantees but with a call to audacious action, reminding rulers that enduring fortune depends on seizing the moment. Entrepreneurs, too, stand at the threshold of limitless possibility. By defining a legacy grounded in authentic values, executing a well-timed and structured exit, reinventing yourself with purpose, and extending your influence through philanthropy, mentorship, and institutional engagement, you ensure that the principality you built persists—its foundations fortified, its spirit undimmed, its influence echoing across generations. In the end, your legacy becomes not a monument to a single individual, but a living testament to strategic vision, resilient culture, and the transformative power of human endeavor.

Conclusion

As our journey draws to a close, it is time to weave together the threads of Machiavellian wisdom and entrepreneurial practice into a cohesive tapestry. Across fourteen chapters, we have translated the ruthless calculus and timeless insights of *The Prince*—on power, adaptation, alliances, innovation, risk, and legacy—into a strategic playbook tailored for the modern founder. In this concluding chapter, we synthesize those principles for day-to-day application; reaffirm the ethical compass that must guide every maneuver; underscore the imperative of continuous learning; and provide a final checklist and action roadmap to carry these lessons from theory into lasting practice.

Synthesizing Machiavellian Principles for Modern Practice

Machiavelli's enduring masterpiece pivots on a few core insights: power is neither moral nor immutable; perception often outweighs reality; adaptability trumps stagnation; and counsel—both internal and external—sharpens judgment. For the entrepreneur, these translate into strategic imperatives:

1. **Command Perception as a Strategic Asset.** "Men judge generally more by the eye than by the hand," Machiavelli writes. In practice, your brand, messaging, and leadership persona shape stakeholder beliefs long before products or metrics do. Treat every public statement, product demo, and customer interaction as an opportunity to reinforce the

virtues—courage, competence, integrity—you wish to
embody.

2. **Balance Fox-Like Cunning with Lion-Like Resolve.**
   Effective leaders combine the agility to sense hidden
   threats and opportunities ("the lion to scare wolves, the fox
   to recognize traps") with the decisiveness to execute bold
   moves. Whether negotiating a partnership, pivoting after
   market feedback, or defending against competitive
   incursions, cultivate both analytical finesse and the
   willingness to commit firmly when the moment demands.

3. **Institutionalize Adaptation.** Machiavelli distinguishes new
   from hereditary states, observing that only structures
   designed by a prince himself can withstand turmoil. For
   startups, this means embedding feedback loops, modular
   processes, and ambidextrous teams that pursue both
   exploitation of core strengths and exploration of new
   frontiers. Make renewal a routine, not an emergency.

4. **Forge Alliances Thoughtfully.** No prince rules alone; he
   surrounds himself with loyal armies, wise counselors, and
   supportive families. Likewise, entrepreneurs need formal
   partnerships, advisory boards, and informal networks.
   Negotiate deals with long-term alignment, diversify
   dependencies to avoid single-point failures, and know
   when to retreat from alliances that erode autonomy.

5. **Guard Reputation as Jealously as Capital.** Machiavelli
   warns that fortunes turn swiftly, and only rulers who
   manage perception endure. Prepare for black swans, build
   financial and operational buffers, and develop crisis

protocols that combine transparency with decisive remediation. When missteps occur, acknowledge them promptly, empathize with stakeholders, and overdeliver on corrective measures to convert vulnerability into trust.

6. **Scaffold Success into Institutions.** Personal charisma ignites growth, but processes, SOPs, and second-line leaders sustain it. Document workflows, codify values into rituals, and invest in leadership development to prevent collapse when founders depart. Maintain flexibility within structures so that established institutions never ossify.

7. **Plan the Final Act as Deliberately as the First.** Defining a legacy and exit strategy—whether IPO, sale, or handover—requires the same strategic rigor applied throughout the venture's life. Shape your narrative, align incentives for successors, and design post-exit reinvention pathways that preserve purpose. Extend your influence through philanthropy, mentorship, and thought leadership to ensure your impact ripples beyond any single enterprise.

Taken together, these principles form a dynamic framework: wield power with purpose, adapt relentlessly, build institutions that outlive individuals, and guard reputation as the lifeblood of legitimacy. They compel entrepreneurs to act neither as naive idealists nor as unprincipled opportunists, but as strategic architects of durable enterprises.

The Ethical Compass: Balancing Strategy with Integrity

Machiavelli's reputation as a champion of amoral statecraft overlooks his own caveats: excessive cruelty breeds hatred; betrayal corrodes trust; and legitimacy ultimately rests on the consent of subjects. Modern founders must navigate a similar tension between strategic ruthlessness and ethical stewardship.

1. **Honor Promises That Matter.** While tactical flexibility may demand secrecy or negotiation nuance, core commitments—to employees' livelihoods, customers' safety, and investors' capital—must be kept. Betrayal of foundational promises inflicts wounds that no subsequent gains can fully heal.

2. **Apply "Practical Virtue."** Machiavelli urges princes to appear merciful, faithful, and upright—regardless of inner calculations. Let your company's culture and external behavior reflect genuine care, fairness, and respect. Where strategy dictates a hard line—downsizing, competitive pricing cuts—soften the blow with transparent rationale, generous support, and a clear path forward for those impacted.

3. **Embed Ethical Guards.** Establish advisory councils or ethics boards charged with vetting new initiatives—beyond compliance checklists—to examine social, environmental, and human impact. This institutionalizes moral oversight and prevents strategic pursuits from veering into reputational peril.

4. **Lead by Example.** Your personal integrity sets the tone for the entire organization. Whether in boardroom negotiations or town-hall disclosures, model the behavior you expect—honest communication, accountability, and the humility to admit mistakes. Machiavelli recognized that subjects model themselves on their prince; your teams will follow suit.

By orienting strategy around an ethical core, entrepreneurs achieve both efficacy and esteem—power that commands compliance and loyalty alike.

Continuous Learning: Staying Vigilant and Adaptive

"No enterprise is more likely to fail than one carried out with excessive caution," Machiavelli warns; yet he also insists that "fortune favors the bold" only when backed by preparation. Continuous learning bridges the gap between audacity and wisdom.

1. **Institutionalize Reflection.** Schedule regular retrospectives across all initiatives—product launches, marketing campaigns, partnership deals—to examine what worked, what failed, and why. Document insights in a shared knowledge base that informs future decisions.

2. **Cultivate Diverse Counsel.** Advisors, mentors, and frontline employees each perceive different facets of reality. Create cross-functional councils that surface

contrarian views, market signals, and emerging trends before they calcify into strategic surprises.

3. **Monitor the "Edge."** Stay attuned to adjacent industries, regulatory shifts, and technological breakthroughs. Machiavelli's princes kept spies to sense threats; modern founders subscribe to industry newsletters, pilot emerging platforms, and participate in think-tanks to detect early ripples.

4. **Promote Experimentation.** Maintain an "innovation portfolio" of hypotheses under test—new features, channels, or business models—evaluated through rapid experiments. Celebrate prudent failures as learning milestones, and institutionalize the "fail fast, learn faster" ethos.

5. **Invest in Personal Growth.** Founders' mindsets shape organizational culture. Commit to continuous education—peer networks, executive programs, or self-directed study of history and philosophy—to expand perspective and reinforce the agility required to navigate uncertainty.

Through relentless learning, entrepreneurs ensure that adaptation remains not a reactive scramble but a proactive capability woven into the enterprise's DNA.

Final Checklist and Action Roadmap

To translate these concluding insights into concrete progress, use the following checklist and roadmap as your guide. Tackle each item deliberately, assigning owners, deadlines, and success metrics to embed Machiavellian practices across your organization.

1. **Strategic Perception Audit**

   - Review all external-facing messaging, product narratives, and leadership communications.

   - Identify any gaps between intended brand virtues and current perceptions.

   - Develop a three-month plan to reinforce desired attributes through coordinated campaigns.

2. **Adaptation Infrastructure**

   - Map existing feedback loops—customer insights, operational dashboards, market intelligence.

   - Close gaps by appointing "intelligence champions" and deploying automated alert systems.

   - Embed quarterly adaptation reviews into the executive calendar.

3. **Alliance Portfolio Review**

- Inventory all active partnerships, joint ventures, and sponsor relationships.

- Assess each for strategic alignment, performance, and dependency risk.

- Develop a realignment plan: deepen high-value alliances, restructure or exit misaligned ones.

4. **Reputation Resilience Plan**

- Finalize crisis management charters and communication templates.

- Conduct a "tabletop exercise" simulating a major service outage or data breach.

- Integrate learnings into updated playbooks and cross-functional training.

5. **Institutionalization Roadmap**

- Document top ten critical processes and designate process owners.

- Launch a living SOP repository with version control and audit schedules.

- Identify high-potential leaders and initiate succession development tracks.

6. **Innovation Ambidexterity Setup**

   - Define exploitation vs. exploration teams, budgets, and governance.

   - Establish an innovation lab or skunkworks charter with autonomy and integration pathways.

   - Schedule biannual hackathons and crowdsourcing initiatives linked to strategic themes.

7. **Growth Strategy Calibration**

   - Revisit horizontal and vertical expansion plans against current capabilities.

   - Conduct market diligence for one target geography or adjacent category.

   - Prepare a 100-day integration plan outline for a hypothetical acquisition or partnership.

8. **Exit Readiness Framework**

   - Clarify personal and organizational objectives for exit—IPO, sale, or handover.

   - Audit financial statements, governance structures, and legal documents for transaction readiness.

- o Develop a succession protocol and post-exit reinvention plan for founders.

9. **Legacy and Influence Blueprint**

   - o Craft a Founder's Manifesto capturing core values and intended long-term impact.

   - o Map philanthropic and mentorship initiatives aligned with personal passions and societal needs.

   - o Outline thought-leadership activities—publishing, speaking, academic affiliations—to extend influence.

10. **Ethics and Integrity Safeguards**

   - o Form or refresh an ethics advisory council with cross-board and functional representation.

   - o Review all major policies—data use, labor practices, supplier standards—and strengthen where needed.

   - o Launch a "culture check" survey to gauge authenticity of ethical commitments and remedy gaps.

With this roadmap, the Machiavellian principles we have distilled—on power, perception, adaptability, alliances, innovation, risk, and legacy—become living practices, not merely chapters in a book. As you implement each step, remember Machiavelli's exhortation that "the best fortress which a prince can possess is the affection of his people." May your principality—your enterprise—stand fortified by the loyalty of customers, the dedication of teams, and the respect of stakeholders, enduring long after any one leader has passed the mantle.

THIS IS NOT A COLLECTION

This volume is part of **Ancient Wisdom Hacks**—
an ongoing body of work focused on how strategy, power, and
failure actually function under pressure.

The books are only one layer.

What you are reading is an entry point into a larger system of
interpretation, application, and expansion.

WHAT THESE WORKS ARE DESIGNED TO DO

Most people look for answers.

These works expose patterns:

- How decisions are made before they are visible
- How systems weaken before they collapse
- How power shifts before it is recognized

This is not theory.
It is applied observation.

THE SYSTEM BEHIND THE WORK

Across all volumes and future releases, three forces remain
constant:

- **Strategy** — how outcomes are shaped before action
- **Conflict** — how people and systems break under pressure
- **Power** — how control is gained, maintained, and lost

No single book contains the full picture.
Each adds another angle.

CONTINUE BEYOND THIS VOLUME

New interpretations, applied volumes, and extended works are
released continuously.

To access current and future material, visit:

www.AncientWisdomHacks.com

WHAT YOU WILL FIND

- Additional applied volumes across industries
- Expanded interpretations of foundational texts
- New releases not available through standard distribution
- Future projects extending beyond books

The system is still expanding.

FINAL POSITION

Clarity does not make outcomes easier.

It removes the illusion that they were ever simple.

Ancient Wisdom Hacks
Interpretation over repetition.
Application over theory.